Not So Different

Teenage attitudes across a decade of change in Northern Ireland

Edited by

Dirk Schubotz and Paula Devine

Russell House Publishing

First published in 2014 by:
Russell House Publishing Ltd.
58 Broad Street
Lyme Regis
Dorset DT7 3QF

Tel: 01297-443948
Fax: 01297-442722
e-mail: help@russellhouse.co.uk
www.russellhouse.co.uk

British Library Cataloguing-in-publication Data:
A catalogue record for this book is available from the British Library.

ISBN: 978-1-905541-92-8

Typeset by TW Typesetting, Plymouth, Devon

Printed by IQ Laserpress, Aldershot

About Russell House Publishing

Russell House Publishing aims to publish innovative and valuable materials to help managers,
practitioners, trainers, educators and students.

Our full catalogue covers: families, children and young people; engagement and inclusion;
drink, drugs and mental health; textbooks in youth work and social work; workforce
development.

Full details can be found at www.russellhouse.co.uk and we are pleased to send out
information to you by post. Our contact details are on this page.

We are always keen to receive feedback on publications and new ideas for future projects.

Contents

Introduction

Paula Devine and Dirk Schubotz

Northern Ireland: Good news/bad news

For the previous five decades people have come to expect that when Northern Ireland is making headline news, it is usually for the wrong reasons: news from Northern Ireland is usually bad news! Thousands have died in the Northern Ireland conflict – the so called *'Troubles'* – since 1969. At the worst times of the conflict, shootings and bombings were weekly, if not daily, occurrences, not to mention threats, beatings, people being forced from their homes because of their religious backgrounds and other sectarian acts of violence. Since the beginning of the Peace Process, and especially since the ceasefires of the mid-1990s, the news stories have occasionally become more positive. Nobel Peace prizes were awarded to the architects of the Northern Ireland Peace Process, and Northern Ireland has been increasingly seen as a model for a successful transformation of a society coming out of violent conflict. People have started to address the atrocities of the past, although this has inevitably been a slow and oftentimes painful process.

In the very recent past, Northern Ireland has again made headlines with what many people would perceive as 'good news stories': the first visit by an English Queen to Northern Ireland, namely Elizabeth II's visit to Belfast and Enniskillen in 2012; the G8 summit held in the Fermanagh Lakelands in the summer of 2013; the World Police and Fire Games being held in Northern Ireland in the summer of 2013; and the fact that Derry/Londonderry became the first UK City of Culture, also in 2013. Young people will undoubtedly also remember that the *MTV Music Awards* ceremony was held in Belfast in November 2011.

Although every single one of these events has attracted some valid criticism, what is important here to note is that they have all been constructed and interpreted in the media as symbolic evidence that Northern Ireland is on a successful path of reconciliation and peace building, without which these events would not have happened. In spite of this, what people will probably remember most are the bad news headlines which again dominated the negativity and unrest around the 12th July Orange parades, and even more so the protests and violence that followed the decision by the Belfast City Council in December 2012 to reduce the flying of the *Union Jack* to a few dedicated days a year. So, in many ways, news on current affairs in Northern Ireland reflects the fact that the transformation from a society deeply affected by socio-religious division and subsequent violent conflict to a peaceful society is often a matter of two steps forward and one step back. Whilst progress has undeniably been made in the past two decades, much more reconciliation work needs to be done.

Finding out what young people think about the changes

But how do young people perceive the changes over the past 15 years? Whilst growing up in a society coming out of conflict sets adolescents from Northern Ireland apart from their counterparts in other parts of the UK, a 16 year old in Belfast deals with the same issues, relating to adolescence, and the developments and decisions young people face *en route* to adulthood as do their counterparts in London, Edinburgh or Cardiff. What is common to adolescents anywhere is that they will seek to find a place as an increasingly equal partner among adults in the societies and communities where they live. For young people in Western democracies this involves decisions about education and employment; negotiations around personal relationships; as well as the continued desire to spend leisure time with friends and peers. How well adolescents manage this process depends on several factors, including the macro-economic conditions in which they live. Adolescence is therefore a stressful time of transition, and some young people deal with this better than others. What young people in Northern Ireland share with their counterparts in other parts of the UK is the negativity that they often experience in the media and in their neighbourhoods during this time of transition. Young people are much more associated – either as perpetrators or victims – with substance misuse, violence, promiscuity, risk-taking and anti-social behaviour than with the positive contribution they make to society, for example as volunteers, informal carers, or as creative artists.

In this volume we review social attitudes and experiences of young people collected in the decade from 2003 to 2012. Over that time, the social policy context has also changed dramatically in Northern Ireland, not least as the political institutions appear to have found their feet. Northern Ireland has now had stable devolved power-sharing government for more than six years. Parallel to these political and policy developments, there has been a general increase in interest in young people's issues in Northern Ireland. The establishment of the Office of the *Northern Ireland Commissioner for Children and Young People* (NICCY) in 2003 has undoubtedly brought children's and young people's issues more to the forefront of policy making in Northern Ireland. Although there has been a plethora of statutory, charitable and voluntary organisations working in Northern Ireland that lobby and provide services for young people, the establishment of NICCY has given that sector more power to influence policy making more directly. NICCY has commissioned a range of research projects on – and often actively involving – children and young people. Some of these were undertaken by ARK using the social attitude survey discussed in this book. The latest example of this is the recent report by the *Ministerial Advisory Group on the Advancement of Shared Education* (Connolly, Purvis and O'Grady, 2013). In this case, NICCY funded ARK to survey 16 year olds, and also 10–11 olds via the *Kids Life and Times* (KLT) survey, to collect children and young people's opinions on more sharing in the divided Northern Irish school sector (For more information on shared education, see Paula Devine's chapter on community relations within this book).

Poverty and austerity

Poverty, and in particular, child poverty, has been the focus of government policy for some time and, in 2006, culminated in the publication of *Lifetime Opportunities*, Government's *Anti-Poverty and Social Inclusion Strategy for Northern Ireland*, and *Improving Children's Life Chances – Child Poverty Strategy* in 2011. It is important to mention that the past decade covered here has seen a very significant change in Britain and Ireland in that a very prosperous period at the start of the new millennium was superseded by a period of financial and economic crisis and austerity which put significant pressure on public and private budgets, some of which will have affected the way young people perceive their life chances.

Of course, many of the people who are directly affected by these policies – namely, children and young people – are not part of the decision-making process. In particular, whilst 16 year olds can be active citizens in many ways (for example, by paying taxes) they cannot participate fully as they cannot vote until they are 18 years of age. More recently, however, there has been much impetus to lower the voting age to 16; see for example, www.votesat16.org/

The scope of this book

This book will address some of these issues. The contributions are based on data collected by the Young Life and Times (YLT) survey, which is undertaken by ARK on an annual basis. ARK is a joint initiative by academics from the two

Northern Ireland universities – Queen's University Belfast and the University of Ulster. In its current format, the YLT survey has collected data on the views, attitudes and experiences of 16 year olds on a range of issues that affect them since 2003. This makes the YLT survey the longest running cross-sectional annual attitude survey among young people in the UK or Ireland. The YLT survey is thus quite unique as it is a reliable, robust and on-going project which allows us to monitor if, and how, attitudes and behaviour change over time. A core set of questions are included in each survey year, such as questions on identity, education, health, and views on politics and sectarianism. A range of other topics are asked less frequently. Significantly, each year YLT also includes a number of questions proposed by the previous year's respondents. Whilst some of these topics are of particular relevance to young people growing up in Northern Ireland, the majority are pertinent issues for adolescents regardless of where they live. More details about the YLT survey and its content can be found in the **Appendix** at the end of this book.

The contributors to this book are well-known academics and social policy makers, who are recognised experts in their field. The subjects covered in this volume predominantly centre on issues explored by more recent YLT surveys. This present publication follows on from *Young people in post-conflict Northern Ireland* (Schubotz and Devine, 2008) which focussed on the findings of the first five years of the YLT attitude surveys. That volume was published ten years after the signing of the *Good Friday/Belfast Agreement*, but only one year after the Northern Ireland Executive had finally got up and running. In this latest book, some authors will pick up and further develop some of the issues that were discussed in the 2008 publication, such as community relations, sexual health and mental health. Other contributors, however, address new topics which also shine a light on the positive contributions that young people make to society, for example as volunteers. Together with an essay by Ewan Nixon, who provides his personal perspective as a 16 year old, the chapters in this book provide comprehensive and compelling insight into key issues facing young adults today.

Most contributions in this book focus on the findings of the YLT surveys conducted since 2008. Thus it is based on the attitudes and experiences of those who live in Northern Ireland and who are now in their late teens or early twenties – in other words the group of young people that can be regarded as the first post-conflict generation. The first years of their lives coincided with the beginning of the Northern Ireland Peace Process. What most of them have in common is that, unlike their parents and grandparents, they have no active personal memory of the worst conflict-related atrocities, even though they are likely to have come across some form of sectarianism.

The structure of this book

As might be expected, community relations, especially with regard to the two traditional communities in Northern Ireland (Protestant and Catholic) remain a major policy area. However, perhaps reflecting their contested nature, community relations have mostly remained in a policy vacuum. As discussed in **Chapter 1** by **Paula Devine**, the implementation of key strategies, such as *A Shared Future* (OFMDFM, 2005b), has fallen foul of political disagreement. Of course, the population of Northern Ireland has changed dramatically over the past ten years, not least because of immigration due to the widening of the European Union. Thus, the first *Racial Equality Strategy* for Northern Ireland was published in 2005. Indeed, the term *community relations* has now been replaced by the term *good relations* to reflect this growing diversity. It is within this context that Paula Devine explores perceptions of, and attitudes to, community relations. Questions have been asked on these topics since 2003, providing the opportunity to analyse a time series of data and explore how attitudes have changed (or not) over the past decade.

Children's rights have become pivotal within much research, not just in Northern Ireland. There is now a statutory requirement to include young people in decision making on issues that affect their lives. However, in **Chapter 2** on rights and democratic participation, **Katrina Lloyd** and **Dirk Schubotz** explore to what extent young people have actually been involved in meaningful decision-making and in what contexts? What effect does participation have on young people's happiness in school and their health in general? Moreover, are young people aware of their rights, and indeed, are they even interested in contributing to decision-making? What are the factors that determine whether or not young people know about their rights?

Their mental health is one of the 'hottest' topics with regard to young people. Recent UNICEF reports show that the UK is performing badly compared to most Western democracies in terms of young people's mental health. Even more worrying, some urban areas in Northern Ireland 'boast' some of the worst rates of self-harm and completed suicides. Based on his experience of working as a social worker and lecturer in the field of mental health, in **Chapter 3** **Gavin Davidson** relates YLT statistics on mental health, including self-harm and suicidal ideation to social work policy and practice.

Leading on from that chapter, **Mark Shevlin** and **Siobhan Murphy** focus on loneliness among 16 year olds, which is an area that has received much less attention so far. In 2011, the YLT survey incorporated an internationally recognised scale which measures loneliness. This was the first time in the UK that such a scale was used in a random sample of young people and the results presented in **Chapter 4** shed light on how loneliness relates to their mental health and general wellbeing.

The importance of play and leisure in the lives of 16 year olds is often overlooked. In **Chapter 5, Jacqueline O'Loughlin** discusses the time spent on play and leisure activities, as well as inhibiting factors, within the context of relevant legislation. Importantly, this chapter includes a discussion of how meaningful play and leisure are in relation to young people's overall sense of who they are and their personal development.

In 2011, Barnardo's published an extensive report on the sexual exploitation of young people in the UK. Later in the same year, Barnardo's in Northern Ireland published *Not a World Away* a report that focussed predominantly on the sexual risks for vulnerable young people in care homes (Beckett, 2011). However, ARK was commissioned by Barnardo's to ask a general sample of 16 year olds about their experiences of sexual grooming and exploitation, and this YLT data was included in Barnardo's report. Whilst the publication received enormous attention, the policy recommendations which set out ways in which young people could be better protected from sexual predators were not implemented. Two years later, in late summer of 2013, the public in Northern Ireland was shaken by the discovery of its very own large scale sexual exploitation case which exposed how over 20 young people from care homes had been systematically sexually abused. This added to recent high profile cases of sexual abuse in Britain and Ireland and was a stark reminder that Northern Ireland is more similar than different to other parts of the UK with regard to many issues that young people have to face. In **Chapter 6, Helen Beckett** analyses and reflects on YLT data on the experiences of sexual grooming and sexual exploitation.

Much of the popular media focuses upon the negative aspects and activities of teenagers, and in fact often views young people as a problem. In contrast, **Chapter 7** by **Christine Irvine** and **Wendy Osborne** focuses on the *positive* contributions that 16 year olds make to our society through volunteering. The chapter considers how the notion of the *Big Society* relates to volunteering. Specifically, why do young people volunteer, and what effect has volunteering on their attitudes and experiences, as well as on society as a whole?

A key feature of the YLT project is the participation of young people, not only in completing the questionnaire, but also in suggesting topics for the following year's survey. Whilst academic and policy makers' in-depth analyses of the survey data are useful, it is equally important to understand what 16 year olds themselves make of all this. **Ewan Nixon** has written a personal reflection on his life as a 16 year old, which we publish here in **Chapter 8**. Ewan was a participant in the 2011 YLT survey, and so we are pleased that he added extra depth to the survey data with this essay. As well as outlining the challenges facing young adults, Ewan highlights the influential role that adults can play, both positively and negatively on adolescents at a time when they struggle to find their own space in an adult-dominated world around them.

In our **Conclusion**, we will reflect on the experiences and challenges of running an attitude survey for ten years that aims to make young people's voices heard and to influence policy making.

References

Barnardo's (2011) *Puppet on a String: The Urgent Need to Cut Children Free From Sexual Exploitation.* Barkingside: Barnardo's.

Beckett, H. (2011) *'Not a World Away'. The Sexual Exploitation of Children and Young People in Northern Ireland.* Belfast: Barnardo's.

Connolly, P., Purvis, D. and O'Grady, P.J. (2013) *Advancing Shared Education: Report of the Ministerial Advisory Group.* Belfast: Queen's University Belfast. Accessed Sept. 2013 at: www.qub.ac.uk/schools/SchoolofEducation/MinisterialAdvisoryGroup/Filestore/Fileto upload,382123,en.pdf

OFMDFM (Office of the First Minister and Deputy First Minster) (2005a) *A Practical Equality Strategy for Northern Ireland.* Belfast: OFMDFM. Accessed Sept. 2013 at: www.ofmdfmni.gov. uk/race-equality-strategy.pdf

OFMDFM (Office of the First Minister and Deputy First Minster) (2005b) *A Shared Future: Improving Relations in Northern Ireland.* Belfast: OFMDFM. Accessed Sept. 2013 at: www.ofmdfmni.gov. uk/asharedfuturepolicy2005.pdf

Schubotz, D. and Devine, P. (Eds.) (2008) *Young People in Post-Conflict Northern Ireland. The Past Cannot Be Changed, But The Future Can Be Developed.* Lyme Regis: Russell House Publishing.

Foreword

Patricia Lewsley Mooney – Northern Ireland Commissioner for Children and Young People

I am delighted to have been asked to provide a foreword to this book, marking as it does ten years of the Young Life and Times survey in its current form, which focusses on the experiences and attitudes of young people aged 16 across Northern Ireland.

This survey is a rich and rare resource providing us with an insight into the lives of young people, their thoughts, hopes and concerns. Through it we hear directly from young people across Northern Ireland on a wide range of issues affecting them including the environment, the legacy of the Northern Ireland conflict, poverty, politics, bullying, sexuality, education, health, policing and relationships with family and friends. The fact that there is now ten years of data enables us to see where there have been changes over time and whether things have improved or worsened for young people.

The Office of the Northern Ireland Commissioner for Children and Young People is also celebrating its 10-year anniversary, and we are reviewing what has changed for children and young people over this period. My role, as set out in the legislation establishing my office, is to *'promote and safeguard the rights and best interests of children and young people'* through scrutinising government delivery, providing advice and invoking my powers as and where necessary. I also have a statutory duty to raise awareness of children's rights and to listen to the views of children and young people as I take my work forward.

On many occasions over the past ten years we have engaged with the Young Life and Times survey team to gather the views of young people. We have commissioned questions on young people's awareness of children's rights, shared education, experiences of age-related discrimination and bullying. We have also used the data collected through the survey to inform our work on other issues, such as attitudes to politics and mental and emotional health. This information has informed my advice to government, providing an insight into the reality of young people's lives and how they feel about the critical issues affecting them.

As the Commissioner for Children and Young People, I am very keen to promote a greater awareness of the right of children and young people to have a say on decisions affecting them, and to have their opinions taken into account in accordance with their age and maturity (Article 12 of the UN Convention on the Rights of the Child). Too often children and young people are marginalised in decision-making processes, not solely through their exclusion from voting, and the associated interest of political parties to win their votes. More often they are excluded through an adult paternalism that, while seeking to protect them, silences their 'voices'. There is also the perception that young people may not have anything valuable to contribute, or that they may lack understanding of the issues – the evidence in this book proves the opposite.

It is essential that those developing policies, legislation and services recognise that engaging directly with children and young people is not an option, or even 'good practice'. It is *essential* both to fulfil their right to be heard, but also to support the development of better policies, legislation and services. Moreover, participation is not realised after hearing from young people, nor even when their views are taken into account and action taken. Young people are a tremendous resource for our society, albeit, too often, an undervalued and marginalised one. We need to understand young people, not as a problem to be solved, but a rich source of potential, with energy, hope and drive. As Kofi Annan has stated:

> *Young people should be at the forefront of global change and innovation. Empowered, they can be key agents for development and peace. If, however, they are left on society's margins, all of us will be impoverished. Let us ensure that all young people have every opportunity to participate fully in the lives of their societies.*

The Young Life and Times survey has provided consistent evidence of the 'lived reality' of young people's lives in Northern Ireland, and of their huge desire and potential to play a part in changing things for the better.

I commend this book to you, and ask that you listen closely to the young people's experiences and opinions contained within it.

About the Authors

The Editors
Paula Devine is Deputy Director of ARK and is based at the School of Sociology, Social Policy and Social Work at Queen's University Belfast.

Dirk Schubotz is Young Life and Times Director of ARK. He is a lecturer in Social Policy at the School of Sociology, Social Policy and Social Work at Queen's University Belfast.

The Contributors
Helen Beckett is Deputy Director of the International Centre for the Study of Sexually Exploited and Trafficked Young People at the University of Bedfordshire.

Gavin Davidson is a lecturer in Social Work and is based at the School of Sociology, Social Policy and Social Work at Queen's University Belfast.

Christine Irvine is Senior Policy and Information Officer at *Volunteer Now*.

Patricia Lewsley Mooney is Northern Ireland's Commissioner for Children and Young People.

Katrina Lloyd is Kids' Life and Times Director of ARK. She is lecturer at the School of Education at Queen's University Belfast.

Siobhan Murphy is a student of Psychology at the University of Ulster.

Ewan Nixon was a respondent to the 2012 Young Life and Times survey. He was 16 years of age at the time. He currently is a final year student at Lagan College, Northern Ireland's first and longest established planned integrated school.

Jacqueline O'Loughlin is Chief Executive of *PlayBoard*, Northern Ireland's leading NGO for Play.

Wendy Osborne (OBE) is Chief Executive of *Volunteer Now*.

Mark Shevlin is Professor at the School of Psychology at the University of Ulster.

Acknowledgements

An annual survey such as the Young Life and Times (YLT) does not run in isolation, and is very much a team effort. The survey would not have run over the last decade without our three ARK colleagues – Lizanne Dowds, Katrina Lloyd and Gillian Robinson. We particularly want to acknowledge and remember the late Professor Ed Cairns from the School of Psychology, University of Ulster, who was a founder member of the YLT management team until his untimely death in 2012, and co-author of a chapter in the previous YLT book. Ed provided so much enthusiasm and support for the survey over the years. As always, we are also grateful for the support from Mike McCool who provides significant technical assistance in managing both the YLT survey and YLT as an online research resource, and for the administrative and secretarial support from Ann Marie Dorrity, Eileen Gray and Shonagh Higgen-botham.

The survey would not have been possible without the many generous funders who have supported the YLT survey since its inception, including the Department of Education for Northern Ireland (DENI); the Economic and Social Research Council; the Electoral Commission; the EU Programme for Peace and Reconciliation in Northern Ireland and the Border Region of Ireland 2000–04, Measure 2:1 – Reconciliation for Sustainable Peace; Northern Ireland Commissioner for Children and Young People (NICCY); the Nuffield Foundation; Office of the First Minister and Deputy First Minister (OFMDFM); and Save the Children.

We would also like to acknowledge the support given by the Department for Social Development and by Her Majesty's Revenue and Customs and Inland Revenue in providing the sample for the YLT survey.

The survey cannot exist without participants, and so it is important to acknowledge the vital role that the thousands of participants have played in providing this essential data source on the lives of 16 year olds in Northern Ireland.

We are very grateful for, and encouraged by, the endorsement that the Northern Ireland Commissioner for Children and Young People, Patricia Lewsley Mooney, has given this book by writing a Foreword.

CHAPTER 1

What a Difference a Decade Makes – or Does it? Community Relations in Northern Ireland

Paula Devine

Introduction

History and commemoration are significant features of life in Northern Ireland, and 2012 was the start of a decade of centenary anniversaries in Northern Ireland. These include the signing of the Ulster Covenant, the Easter Uprising, the Battle of the Somme, and the establishment of Northern Ireland, among others. Importantly for this book, 2012 also marked the 10th year of the Young Life and Times (YLT) survey in its current format.

Young people were one of the groups worst affected by past violence and sectarianism in Northern Ireland: four out of ten conflict-related deaths were of young people under the age of 24 years (Fay, Morrisey and Smyth, 1999). Between 1969 and 1998, 257 young people under the age of 18 years died as a direct result of the conflict, and this figure rose to 324 by 2003. In particular, the impact on young people living in the areas worst affected by the conflict was found to be most acute (Smyth et al., 2004). Whilst such levels and intensity of violence has greatly reduced since then, anecdotal and research evidence indicates that young people are still growing up in a society deeply divided by national and socio-religious identities, in which the world is still divided into 'us' and 'them'.

Throughout the ten years of the survey, important political, policy and demographic changes were taking place in Northern Ireland. However, a review of community relations and the general political situation judged the progress and success of the Peace Process as being ambiguous:

> There are radically opposing views among experts on whether, ten years on, the settlement has reduced or increased sectarianism, as to whether it has crystallised or softened opposing views, and as to whether it has solidified or moderated opposing blocs, or perhaps even begun to transform them.
>
> (Todd, 2009: 348)

Such conflicting evidence on the state of community relations include the visit of Queen Elizabeth II to Dublin in 2011 which was seen as the culmination of a long-term process of reconciliation between British and Irish identities, and the street disorders following the decision of Belfast City Council in December 2012 to restrict the flying of the Union flag above Belfast City Hall to 18 designated days per year.

It is within such a contradictory context that this chapter will focus on young people's attitudes, experience and influences relating to community relations in Northern Ireland. Questions have been asked on these topics within YLT since 2003, providing the opportunity to explore how responses have changed (or not) over the past decade.

Political and policy context

For many, the signing of the Good Friday/Belfast Agreement of 1998 is seen as the end of the conflict (also known as 'The Troubles') although the Peace Process consists of a much wider series of political and policy developments in Northern Ireland. Point 2 of the Good Friday/Belfast Agreement is that negotiators dedicated themselves 'to the achievement of reconciliation, tolerance, and mutual trust, and to the protection and vindication of the human rights of all' (NIO, 1998).

Extensive demilitarisation occurred and many obvious barriers and signs of the Northern Ireland conflict have disappeared since the first ceasefire of paramilitary groups in 1994. Nevertheless, many interface barriers (including walls, gates and security fences) that keep communities apart still exist, known colloquially as *'Peace Walls'*. Recent research among residents living beside Peace Walls has shown that while 76 per cent would like to see these come down now or in the near future, 38 per cent believe that Peace Walls are necessary because of the potential for violence (Byrne, Gormley Heenan and Robinson, 2012). Nevertheless, Leonard and McKnight (2011) endorse the need to take young people's views of Peace Walls into account when assessing the legacy of the conflict in Northern Ireland. Their research with 14 and 15 year olds found that while some were optimistic that Peace Walls could be removed, many teenagers felt that walls and barriers were still needed to keep the two communities apart, 'just in case'.

Whilst devolution was an integral part of the Agreement, this had a stop-start history, and has only been running consistently since May 2007. Mirroring this pattern, community relations policy development in Northern Ireland has also had a sporadic past. *A Shared Future: Improving Relations in*

Northern Ireland was published in 2005 (OFMDFM, 2005). This policy framework, initiated by the direct-rule government in Westminster, made it clear that improving relationships between and within communities in Northern Ireland is a long term goal for Government (Donnan, 2007). However, political wrangling meant that this framework was never endorsed.

After the restoration of devolution in 2007, the Northern Ireland Executive committed itself to the development of a new strategy for community relations in Northern Ireland. After much delay, a new policy framework *A Programme for Cohesion, Sharing and Integration* (OFMDFM, 2010) was released for public consultation, leading to substantial debate and discussion at both political and community levels (Devine, Kelly and Robinson, 2011). However, there was widespread rejection of this consultation paper, not least because it was seen as reinforcing the *status quo* of a divided society.

Since then another policy has been formulated. The *Together: Building a United Community* (TBUC) strategy, published in May 2013 reflects the Northern Ireland Executive's commitment to improving community relations (OFMDFM, 2013). However, whilst this strategy is designed to facilitate a more united and shared society, it explicitly omits the controversial issues of flags, marches and the Parades Commission, which will be dealt with using separate mechanisms. Nevertheless, one of the four key priorities within this strategy is *Children and Young People*, in particular, 'to continue to improve attitudes amongst our young people and to build a community where they can play a full and active role in building good relations' (OFMDFM, 2013: 4). The practical commitments related to this priority include a range of school and community based initiatives, such as a 'buddy scheme' in publicly-run nursery and primary schools, and one year placements for 10,000 young people who are not in education, employment or training (NEET) in a new 'United Youth' volunteering programme. The other key priorities also have relevance to the lives of young people living in Northern Ireland, namely, *Shared Community*, *Safe Community*, and *Cultural Expression*.

Recording the attitudes of young people

The YLT Survey has been collecting the views of 16 year olds on community relations since 2003, providing a unique time series of attitudes. Data from YLT and the Northern Ireland Life and Times (NILT) survey of adults have been included within the set of outcome indicators used to reflect the state of good relations relevant to *A Shared Future* (Donnan, 2007). In addition, YLT data appears within the first *Peace Monitoring Report* (Nolan, 2012) in relation to young people's attitudes to volunteering. (For further analysis of young people and volunteering, see Osborne and Irvine's chapter in this book). Attitudinal data provide a necessary complement to more administratively-based data included in these indicator sets, and give important information 'on the ground' from a wide spectrum of the public who are citizens and voters (or soon to be voters, in the case of 16 year olds). Descriptive findings of attitudes on community relations among young people have been regularly reported (Devine and Schubotz, 2004; Schubotz and Devine, 2005; Schubotz and Robinson, 2006; Morrow, 2008; Schubotz and McCartan, 2008; Devine and Robinson, 2012; Devine and Schubotz, 2012; Devine, 2013) as well as for those among the adult population (Hughes and Donnelly, 2001 and 2003; MacGinty, 2003 and 2004; Hayes, McAllister and Dowds, 2006; Muldoon et al., 2008; Devine, Kelly and Robinson, 2011). Fullerton (2004) provided a comparison of the views of young people and adults. For the first time, however, this chapter takes advantage of a full decade of data to explore young people's attitudes from 2003 to 2012.

By 2012, 14 years had passed since the signing of the Good Friday/Belfast Agreement in 1998, and the Northern Ireland Executive had been functioning in its present form since May 2007. So whilst there have been radical political changes, with Sinn Féin now sharing power with the Democratic Unionist Party (DUP) which would have been inconceivable in the past, has this translated into improved perceptions of relationships between the two main communities in Northern Ireland? There are two, often contradictory, schools of thought about the future of community relations. The first is that, as time goes on, there will be a reduction in community differences and divisions, especially among those young people who did not live through the height of the violent conflict. The second is that these political, cultural and religious differences are so deeply embedded that they will not easily change. The result is a continuation of segregated lives and sectarian views within the context of a 'separate but equal' existence (Devine, Kelly and Robinson, 2011). However, is either of these views borne out in the survey results?

Perception of community relations

Two key indicators allow us to 'take the temperature' of the state of community relations in Northern Ireland: people's perception of relations between the two main communities over the previous five years, and their perception of relations in the future five years.

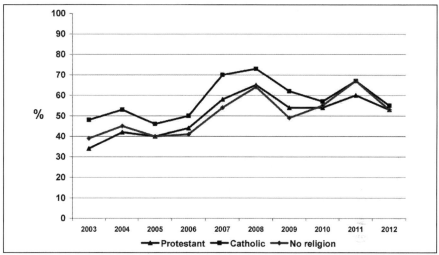

Source: 2003–2012 YLT surveys

Figure 1.1   % believing that relations between Protestants and Catholics are better now than 5 years ago, by religion

Figure 1.1 shows that the proportion of YLT respondents who believe that relations between Protestants and Catholics are better now than five years ago was higher in 2012 (53%) than it was in 2003 (41%). However, there has been much fluctuation over the years which often mirrors contemporary political and policy events. Thus, the high point was in 2008 (68%), perhaps reflecting optimism following the introduction of devolution in the previous year. In contrast, there was a large drop between 2011 and 2012, some of which may be due to tensions around the Belfast City Council flag decision (Devine, 2013). Indeed, one respondent said in 2012 'The community is probably more divided than last year this time as the union flag was taken down from the City Hall'.

Therefore, whilst the overall rise in optimism since 2003 would suggest that we are moving towards a more normalised society characterised by improved community relations, the fluctuations suggest that attitudes are not immune to external events. Given the subject matter, it is apposite to explore if Catholics and Protestants have held similar positions over time, or if the opinions of one group are changing at a different rate or direction to that of the other. Figure 1.1 shows that the upward trend is evident for both Catholic and Protestant respondents, as well as those respondents with no religion. However, two patterns are worth noting. Firstly, whilst Protestant respondents were less positive than those respondents with no religion in 2003 and 2004, this pattern was reversed from 2006 to 2009. This may reflect a general concern at the time that the Peace Process and Good Friday/Belfast Agreement mainly focused on relations between Protestants and Catholics, without giving recognition to those who are neither. On the other hand, it may also be that people identify as having no religion specifically because of their pessimism with Catholic and Protestant identities or the relationship between them (Devine, Kelly and Robinson, 2011). Secondly, attitudes among these three groups have converged – in 2003, there was a difference of 14 percentage points between the most and least positive groups, but this had fallen to three percentage points in 2012.

Turning now to the future, Figure 1.2 shows the proportion of young people who think that relations between Protestants and Catholics will be better in five years time. Of note is the fluctuation since 2008, with some intra-group variations. As with Figure 1.1, Catholics were consistently the most optimistic group, with some swapping of position between Protestants and those with no religion. Again, following the trend in Figure 1.1, the gap between these groups has been decreasing over time. In 2003, there was a difference of 17 percentage points between the proportion of Catholics and the proportion of Protestants believing that community relations will be better in five years time. By 2010, this gap had narrowed to three percentage points, but increased to

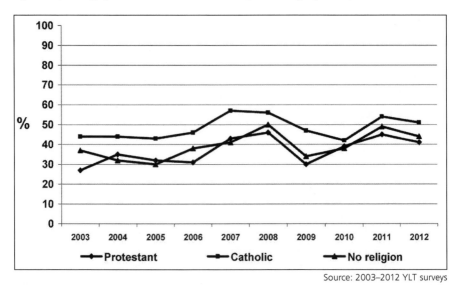

Source: 2003–2012 YLT surveys

Figure 1.2 % believing that relations between Protestants and Catholics will be better in 5 years time, by religion

ten percentage points by 2012. Again, this may reflect recent disturbances relating to Orange Parades and the flag protests (Devine, 2013).

Integrate or segregate?

One major feature of life in Northern Ireland is segregation in relation to where people live, go to school, work or socialise. However, is the increasing drive within government policy towards sharing and integration over the last few years reflected in public attitudes?

In 2003, around one in ten YLT respondents (9%) attended schools that they described as religiously mixed, that is, about half Protestant and half Catholic. Included in this figure are the six per cent of respondents who attended a planned integrated school. The latter are schools that were specifically set up with an integrated ethos and require an intake of at least 40 per cent of the minority community within the specific area. By 2012, nearly six out of ten respondents (15%) attended religiously-mixed schools, although the proportion attending integrated schools was similar to 2003. This suggests a rise in the number of schools that have a mixed school population by virtue of their academic reputation or the residential composition of their catchment area. Interestingly, the proportion of respondents saying that they did not know the religious mix of their school had risen from one per cent to six per cent in the decade from 2003.

At the same time, there has been a small increase in the proportion of young people saying that they lived in mixed-religion neighbourhoods, from 29 per cent in 2003 to 35 per cent in 2012. This means that one in six YLT respondents still live in an area in which most of their neighbours are either predominantly Catholic or predominantly Protestant. Therefore, residential and educational segregation remain the norm.

However, just because young people may have no choice but to live and be educated within a segregated environment, does this mean that they would personally choose this situation? Figure 1.3 suggests that support for integration within the workplace has been consistently strong, with residential integration less so. Indeed, support for residential integration has fallen more recently, from 65 per cent in 2011 to 56 per cent in 2012. However, integrated schools are only welcomed by around one half of respondents. What is very striking is that for all three scenarios (neighbourhood, workplace and school), the figures for 2012 are very similar to that for 2003, despite some fluctuation during the intervening years.

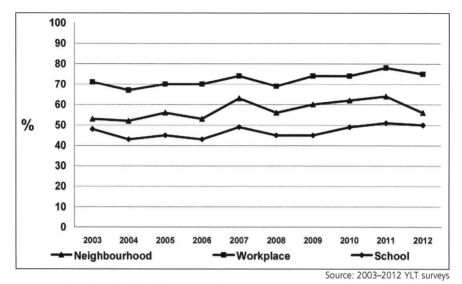

Source: 2003–2012 YLT surveys

Figure 1.3   % supporting religious mixing

This graph belies the varying attitudes among those in different groups. Perhaps unsurprisingly, respondents with no religion were the most strongly supportive of mixing in all three environments (neighbourhood, workplace and school). Catholics consistently have been the least likely to want their children educated in mixed-religion schools. With the exception of 2010, Protestant respondents were least likely to want to live in mixed-religion neighbourhoods, or have mixed-religion workplaces. What is also interesting is the similarity of attitudes in relation to workplace integration, with only four percentage points between the groups in both 2003 and 2012. However, in relation to education, there has consistently been a gap of at least 30 percentage points, showing the variation in attitudes between these groups. No doubt, some of this is due to the complex and segregated nature of the education system in Northern Ireland. In 2012/13, 44 per cent of pupils in Northern Ireland attended schools that were within the remit of the Council for Catholic Maintained Schools (DENI, 2013). Given their experience of schools wherein the vast majority of pupils are Catholic, it may explain why Catholic respondents are more supportive of schools with pupils of their own religion.

Education policy

These findings indicate that segregation of schools is an issue that will continue to be divisive. Several strategies have been implemented within education over the past 30 years with the express aim of improving community relations: new curricular programmes and textbooks; cross-community contact initiatives; and development of integrated schools. However, the impact of some of these has been mixed (Gallagher et al., 2010).

When the YLT survey began in 2003, integrated education was seen as the only alternative to a segregated education structure. Since then, there have been several policy initiatives that have come to the fore. In particular, the concept of Shared Education has been developed, and much policy and research work has focused on the potential of this new system as a way of improving community relations. Indeed, within the 2013 TBUC strategy, there is a commitment to develop ten new shared education campuses, to enhance the quality and extent of shared education provision (OFMDFM, 2013). This is seen as a mechanism to ensure that sharing in education becomes a central part of every child's educational experience.

Within Shared Education, the make-up of individual schools does not change; instead, each school develops links with other schools and develops joint classes or projects, or shared facilities. One definition is that it:

> . . . involves two or more schools or other educational institutions from different sectors working in collaboration with the aim of delivering educational benefits to learners, promoting the efficient and effective use of resources, and promoting equality of opportunity, good relations, equality of identity, respect for diversity and community cohesion.
>
> (Connolly, Purvis and O'Grady, 2013: xiii)

Or, as Nolan (2012: 127) describes it:

> The shared education approach accepts a religious divided school system, but tries to make the walls more porous by encouraging practical co-operation.

Extensive school-based and research initiatives include the Sharing Education Programme which began in 2007 to support schools in the formation of cross-sectoral partnerships in order to provide enhanced educational opportunities for students (see www.schoolsworkingtogether.co.uk/). Of relevance to community relations, is that this programme also promotes reconciliation by facilitating collaboration and sharing between the schools, in particular focusing on the provision of sustained, high-quality curricular activities. A Ministerial Advisory Group on the Advancement of Shared Education was set up and reported in early 2013 (see www.qub.ac.uk/schools/SchoolofEducation/ MinisterialAdvisoryGroup/). Importantly, the final report of that body (Connolly, Purvis and O'Grady, 2013) made extensive use of the research on attitudes of children and young people, some of which had been recorded using questions within the 2012 YLT and Kids' Life and Times (KLT) survey of 10/11 year olds. These questions were funded by the Office of the Northern Ireland Commissioner for Children and Young People (NICCY).

Overall, doing projects and sharing facilities and classes with pupils from other schools was seen by the YLT and KLT respondents as a good idea. Furthermore, reaction among those who had already participated in shared education activities was positive (Lloyd, 2013; NICCY, 2013). However, their concerns included being bullied, having to mix with pupils from a different religious background, and the appropriateness of pupils from grammar and non-grammar schools engaging in shared activities and classes. One of the four key priorities within the *Together: Building a United Community* strategy is a *Safe Community*. Thus, the advancement of shared education will need to take these issues on board before young people can feel truly safe within such an environment (Lloyd, 2013).

The Department of Education in Northern Ireland (DENI) has introduced a Community Relations, Equality and Diversity in Education (CRED) policy. The aim of CRED is to help improve relations between communities by educating children and young people to develop self-respect and respect for others, promote equality and work to eliminate discrimination, and by providing formal and non-formal education opportunities for them to build relationships with those of different backgrounds and traditions within the resources available. Given the specific remit of DENI, this policy covers both formal (school) and informal (youth project and youth club) settings. Questions exploring experiences and attitudes towards this policy were included in the 2012 YLT survey. Overall, the data indicate that the majority of young people are experiencing CRED activities in some shape or form, and these seem effective in changing attitudes. The fact that the breadth and range, as well as perceived effectiveness, may vary across settings is evident. However, this may be expected, given the different roles that schools and youth projects/clubs play within young people's lives (Devine, 2013a).

Feelings about others

Having so far looked at the macro level of community relations more generally, have there been any changes in how young people themselves feel about people from other traditions? The following quote from a YLT respondent in 2011 suggests a blurring of the traditional 'us and them' categories of Catholic and Protestant, and reflects how much Northern Ireland society has changed since 2003.

It is difficult to answer a question about what religion of people you prefer to be around or what race you prefer to be around because I feel that this does not reflect my view that I choose to be around, or not be around, someone as a result of their personality not what their race or religion is.

Starting with the 'traditional' religious divide, Devine and Robinson (2012) found a complicated picture of how favourable young people feel about those from a different religious community. Since 2003, the proportion of respondents feeling 'favourable' has stayed the same or decreased. However, it is not the case that respondents feel 'unfavourably' about people from particular communities; instead, there has been a rise in the proportion saying that they feel 'neither favourable nor unfavourable' towards people who are either Catholic or Protestant (see Table 1.1). This may indicate that young people prefer not to make a judgement on an entire group of people from a particular community. Instead, they may be making decisions based on the individual person, rather than their community background – a point made in the comment above.

Who is the other?

Of course, Northern Ireland society has changed greatly since 2003. In particular, the expansion of the European Union and other social, economic and political changes on a global level, have resulted in a previously unseen level of immigration to Northern Ireland. The 2001 Census of Population indicated that 0.8 per cent of the Northern Ireland population had an ethnicity other than 'white', and 1.8 per cent of the population were born outside the United Kingdom or Ireland. By 2011, these figures were 1.8 per cent and 4.5 per cent respectively (see www.nisra.gov.uk/Census.html). While small in absolute numbers, this change in the population has resulted in the term '*good relations*' being used instead of '*community relations*' to reflect this growing diversity. However, attitudes towards these incoming groups are mixed, as indicated by these comments in 2011:

I think it's good that more ethnic minority groups are coming into Ireland and should be welcomed among schools and local communities.

Too many foreigners in our country – no job prospects for us!

Table 1.1 Feelings about people from different religious communities

%

	Feeling about Catholic community			Feeling about Protestant community		
	Part of the Protestant community	Part of the Catholic community	Neither	Part of the Protestant community	Part of the Catholic community	Neither
2003						
Favourable	38	77	47	74	45	48
Neither favourable nor unfavourable	49	20	50	25	43	50
Unfavourable	11	1	2	1	9	2
2012						
Favourable	38	75	30	68	42	29
Neither favourable nor unfavourable	52	22	65	31	51	64
Unfavourable	8	1	1	2	4	2

Source: 2003 and 2012 YLT surveys

In 2004, when the question was first asked, 40 per cent of YLT respondents said that they felt favourable about people from minority ethnic communities, and nearly one half (48%) said they felt neither favourable nor unfavourable. Since then, the proportion feeling favourable has fluctuated over time, dropping to 30 per cent in 2005, and rising to 46 per cent in 2012.

Cross-community contact

So far, this chapter has focused on attitudes. This next section looks at behaviour in terms of cross-community contact. Those respondents who considered that they were part of the Protestant or Catholic community were asked about their contact with people from the 'other' community. In both 2003 and 2011, around two thirds of these young people said that they had participated in a cross-community project, and the vast majority had positive feelings about these activities.

In 2012, just under one third (31%) of respondents from a Protestant or Catholic community background said that they very often socialise or play sport with people from a different religious community from themselves. A further 29 per cent did do sometimes, whilst 37 per cent rarely or never do so. Table 1.2 shows that in 2003, 46 per cent of 16 year olds said that they rarely or never do this, indicating a rise in this type of cross-community contact. In both 2003 and 2011, these patterns were similar among respondents who were members of the Catholic or Protestant communities, although for 2012, the 'very often' figure was higher for Protestants than for Catholics.

As we might expect, young people who had attended an integrated school

Table 1.2 How often do you socialise or play sport with people from (a) a different religious community to yourself? (b) a different ethnic background to yourself?

		%		
	Different religious community		Different ethnic background	
	2003	2012	2008	2011
Very often	27	31	13	19
Sometimes	25	29	31	36
Rarely	27	23	33	26
Never	19	14	21	16
Don't know	1	3	2	3

Source: YLT surveys, 2003–2011

were most likely to say that they very often socialised or played sport with people from a different religious community: 55 per cent, compared with 35 per cent of those attending a grammar school and 22 per cent of those attending a secondary school in 2012. In addition, young people who have taken part in cross-community projects were more likely to socialise or play sport with people from a different religious community (33% did so very often, compared with 26% who had not participated in cross-community projects).

The YLT surveys in 2008 and in 2011 included questions about contact with people from a minority ethnic group. The results show a slight rise in the proportion of respondents who said that they socialise or play sport with people from a minority ethnic group *very often* or *sometimes*, along with a corresponding decrease in the percentage who *never* do. However, in 2011, there was less frequent contact with people from ethnic minority groups than with people from a different religious community: 66 per cent of respondents *very often* or *sometimes* socialise or play sport with people from a different religious community compared with only 55 per cent doing so with people from a different ethnic background. Matching the pattern seen earlier, respondents attending integrated schools were more likely to socialise or play sport with people from a different ethnic background.

Cross-community friendship

Of course, we need to acknowledge that many cross-community activities (especially sport) take place within a school setting and are not necessarily the choice of the participants. Thus, they may not result in long-term cross-community contact and friendship. Therefore, it is important to explore more informal friendship patterns. There has been a fall in the proportion of those YLT respondents who are part of the Catholic or Protestant community saying that they did not have any friends from the other main religious community: from 33 per cent in 2003 to 24 per cent in 2012. Devine and Robinson (2012) identified higher levels of cross-community friendship among young people attending integrated schools, as well as among those who had participated in a cross-community scheme.

Making friends with someone from a different background is especially difficult in a segregated society, when the opportunity to meet other people is limited, and this is highlighted in O'Loughlin's chapter within this book looking at play and leisure. In addition, public perceptions, stereotypes and fears are also impediments to cross-community friendship, as highlighted by a YLT respondent in 2012 'People tend to stereotype ethnic minorities and are afraid to come into contact with them'.

In 2011, one quarter (26%) said that *all* of their friends were of the same race or ethnic origin as themselves, and a further 60 per cent said that *most* of their friends were. When first asked in 2006, around one half of respondents (48%) said that *all* their friends were of the same race or ethnic origin. These figures suggest that young people are mixing more with people from different backgrounds, and reflecting this, one young person in 2012 said: 'It doesn't matter what your religion or colour is: I have loads of friends and religion and colour never comes into it'.

Of course, it is important to ask whether these experiences are any different for young people living in Britain or in Ireland, where residential and educational segregation also exists? Cassidy, O'Connor and Dorrer (2006) explored the social networks of secondary school pupils in Glasgow. One key finding was that Pakistani and white participants reported significantly higher numbers of network members from their own ethnic group than participants from Indian and Chinese backgrounds. Reasons for these patterns include the particular ethnic background of individual schools and neighbourhoods. This suggests that the impact of educational and residential segregation is as prevalent elsewhere as it is in Northern Ireland.

Why think like this?

So far in this chapter, we have seen how young people rate the current and future state of community relations in Northern Ireland, as well as their level of support towards integration. When compared with responses from the NILT survey of adults aged 18 years or over, one key finding is that YLT respondents tend to be less positive than NILT respondents with regard to perceptions of relations – both looking back and into the future. This seems somewhat at odds with what might be expected, given that these young people have not lived through the worst of the conflict. Furthermore, we should also ask whether the lack of unanimous support for integration amongst 16 year olds is indeed due to an explicit wish for religious or cultural segregation, or rather due to lack of experience of an alternative system. After all, the vast majority of YLT respondents have been educated all their lives within a mainly segregated school system. Moreover, the opportunities for young people to extend their friendship groups beyond the immediate neighbourhood environ-ment, which, as discussed above, for the majority of young people are single-religion settings, can be limited. Adults, on the other hand, frequently interact with people from different backgrounds in their workplaces, and this is likely to influence their attitudes. The lack of meaningful cross-community contact may have an impact upon the behaviour of some younger people and might be seen as one of the reasons why more pessimistic attitudes exist, and indeed, as has been argued, why some young people get involved in rioting (Harland, 2011).

The fear of being vulnerable to attack may also be pertinent, as a quote from a YLT respondent in 2009 demonstrates: 'I would only prefer to live in a neighbourhood with people from my own religious community to avoid conflict, and to avoid having to live in fear of sectarian attacks'.

Given this concern, it will be a challenge for the TBUC strategy to match the key priorities of a shared community and a safe community.

It is also known that attitudes do not always conclusively predict behaviour, which is borne out by the fact that the proportion of survey respondents who say that they favour religious mixing is significantly higher than the proportion of those who actually experience it. In this case, however, young people do not necessarily have the opportunity to exercise their choice. Thus, Morrow's (2008) contention that community division remains the great structuring principle of Northern Ireland still remains true today.

The transmission of attitudes from one generation to another is also important here, and the survey has consistently asked Protestant and Catholic YLT respondents to identify the most important influence on their views on the other main religious community. Figure 1.4 clearly shows that for all years, the modal response, which accounted for approximately one half of respondents,

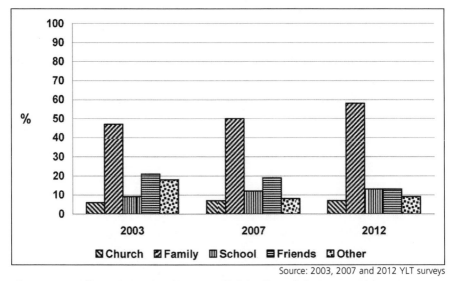

Source: 2003, 2007 and 2012 YLT surveys

Figure 1.4   Influence on attitudes towards the other religious community

was *'my family'*. The next most frequent responses related to *friends* and *school*.

This is reinforced by the comments of YLT respondents:

I think that community relations are improving all the time, and the bitterness between communities stems from our ancestors, so we must not allow their views on community relations to be carried onto our children of the future.

(2003)

I don't think relations between Catholics and Protestants will ever really improve because religious prejudices are passed down from parents to their children. Religious hatred is not a natural thing; it is not in-born, it is created by people.

(2007)

I believe sectarianism among people my age would be due to their parents passing their biased opinions down through the generations.

(2012)

Linked to this is a strong feeling among young people that religion will always make a difference to the way people think about each other in Northern Ireland, although this has fallen from 86 per cent in 2003 to 77 per cent in 2012. At the same time, respondents have become slightly more equivocal, with a rise in the proportion giving 'other' answers or saying that they don't know. Several of these young people highlighted that politics or history are more important than religion, for example:

I feel that it is politics which divides N.I. not religion.

(2012)

It's not so much about religion no more, religion is just labelling it – it's more about the past, and previous actions and behaviours.

(2012)

Discussion

The aim of this chapter was to explore the attitudes among 16 year olds to community relations in Northern Ireland over the past ten years, particularly to examine if changes in attitudes have kept pace with political change over the same period. Given that the young people who took part in these surveys grew up in relatively peaceful times, it might be expected that they would be optimistic about the future and more supportive of mixing in everyday life.

So has a decade made a difference? Reflecting on Morrow's (2008) previous analysis of YLT data from 2003 to 2007, the data presented in this chapter suggests that the answer to this question isn't straightforward. Firstly, there has been a notable convergence of attitudes between Catholic and Protestant respondents over time. Secondly, while the overall trend in community relations over the ten-year period from the first YLT survey to the most recent one in 2012 has been positive, the peak in optimism was in 2008. In fact, 16 year olds' levels of optimism about community relations in the future were very similar in 2003 and 2012. As argued above, these data are reflective of, and influenced by, contemporary events. As one respondent to the 2009 survey noted:

> Northern Ireland is on a slippery slope with regards community relations. Sectarian violence is on the rise again, social tensions are growing and young and old feel disillusioned with the parties in the assembly. These politicians do not want to see an equal Northern Ireland, because their very support base is centred around sectarian beliefs.

Young people still experience high levels of educational and residential segregation and, at the same time, are more likely than their adult counterparts to support continued segregation. Previous analysis (Devine and Schubotz, 2010) showed that experience of segregation and strength of national and religious identity was strongly associated with support for segregation. Because attitudes are known not to conclusively instigate actions, at this point it is impossible to say whether or not the 16 year olds of today will actually choose to live or work in environments that are more or less divided. This appears to be a 'chicken and egg' situation – which comes first: *support* for segregation or *experience* of segregation? This is the challenge facing government policy. However, the continuous development of social policy interventions may mean that young people will live in a more shared society in Northern Ireland in the future. Of particular note are developments in Shared Educaton and also the new priorities expressed within the *Together: Building a United Community* strategy.

As society is changing, so are friendship and social networks. Sixteen year olds in Northern Ireland increasingly have contact across both the religious and ethnic divides. Only a minority of young people report having no friends from other backgrounds, and this is a significant change since 2003. Comments made by some YLT respondents reinforce the idea that friendship is not simply based on religion or ethnicity, but on the person as a whole. However, there is a sense that an 'us and them' mentality still exists, given that 14 per cent of young people never socialise or play sport with people from a different religious community, and 16 per cent never do so with people from a different ethnic background. In addition, 24 per cent have no friends from the other main religious community and 26 per cent say all their friends are the same race or ethnic group as themselves. Thus, the YLT findings present some optimism, but also some challenges, in building a shared community and enhanced cultural expression, as promoted in the current TBUC strategy.

Why is it important to record these attitudes? Sixteen year olds in Northern Ireland, like their counterparts elsewhere in the UK, live in a slightly twilight world. On the one hand, they can leave school, go out to work, earn money and pay taxes. Thus, to all intents and purposes, they are active citizens – but they are citizens without the right to vote. Nevertheless, it is important to take heed of their opinions. Indeed, as McEvoy stressed,

> *It is the currently disenfranchised young (those under 18) who will determine the success or failure of any peace process in the long term.*

(2000: 87)

Thus, their attitudes and perceptions will determine how – or if – they use their vote in the future, and how these votes will impact on community relations in the years to come.

References

Byrne, J., Gormley Heenan, C. and Robinson, G. (2012) *Attitudes to Peace Walls.* Jordanstown: University of Ulster. Accessed Sept. 2013 at: www.ark.ac.uk/peacewalls2012/peacewalls2012.pdf

Cassidy, C., O'Connor, R. and Dorrer, N. (2006) *Young People's Experiences of Transition to Adulthood: A Study of Minority Ethnic and White Young People.* York: Joseph Rowntree Foundation.

Connolly, P., Purvis, D. and O'Grady, P.J. (2013) *Advancing Shared Education: Report of the Ministerial Advisory Group.* Belfast: Queen's University Belfast.

DENI (Department of Education for Northern Ireland) (2013) *Enrolment by School Management Type.* Bangor: DENI. Accessed Sept. 2013 at www.deni.gov.uk/enrolment_by_school_management_type_updated_1213.xls.xlsx

Devine, P. (2013) *Into the Mix.* ARK Research Update 83, Belfast: ARK, Accessed Sept. 2013 at: www.ark.ac.uk/publications/updates/update83.pdf

Devine, P. (2013a) *Community Relations, Equality and Diversity in Education (CRED): Findings from the 2012 Young Life and Times Survey.* Belfast: ARK. Accessed Sept. 2013 at: www.ark.ac.uk/publications/occasional/CREDYLT12.pdf

Devine, P., Kelly, G. and Robinson, G. (2011) *An Age of Change? Community Relations in Northern Ireland.* ARK Research Update 72, Belfast: ARK. Accessed Sept. 2013 at: www.ark.ac.uk/publications/updates/update72.pdf.

Devine, P. and Robinson, G. (2012) *No More 'Us and Them' for 16 Year Olds?* ARK Research Update 79, Belfast: ARK. Accessed Sept. 2013 at: www.ark.ac.uk/publications/updates/update79.pdf

Devine, P. and Schubotz, D. (2004) *Us and Them?* ARK Research Update 28, Belfast: ARK. Accessed Sept. 2013 at: www.ark.ac.uk/publications/updates/update28.pdf.

Devine, P. and Schubotz, D. (2010) Caught up in the Past? The Views of 16-Year Olds on Community Relations in Northern Ireland. *Shared Space: A Research Journal on Peace, Conflict and Community Relations in Northern Ireland,* 10, 5–22.

Devine, P. and Schubotz, D. (2012) Segregation Preferences of Urban and Rural 16-Year Olds in Northern Ireland. *Irish Political Studies,* iFirst 1-23 DOI:10.1080/07907184.2012.729210 Accessed Sept. 2013

Donnan, P. (2007) A Shared Future and Facial Equality Strategy: Good Relations Indicators Baseline Report. *Shared Space: A Research Journal on Peace, Conflict and Community Relations in Northern Ireland,* 4, 5–16.

Fay, M., Morrisey, M. and Smyth, M. (1999) *Northern Ireland's Troubles: The Human Costs.* London: Pluto Press.

Fullerton, D. (2004) *Changing times – or are they?* ARK Research Update 30, Belfast: ARK. Accessed Sept. 2013 at: www.ark.ac.uk/publications/updates/update30.pdf

Gallagher, T. et al. (2010) Sharing Education Through Schools Working Together. *Shared Space: A Research Journal on Peace, Conflict and Community Relations in Northern Ireland,* 10, 65–73.

Harland, K. (2011) Violent Youth Culture in Northern Ireland: Young Men, Violence, and the Challenges of Peacebuilding. *Youth & Society,* 43: 2, 414–32.

Hayes, B.C., McAllister, I. and Dowds, L. (2006) *The Impact of Integrated Education on Political Attitudes in Northern Ireland.* ARK Research Update 42, Belfast: ARK. Accessed Sept. 2013 at: www.ark.ac.uk/publications/updates/update42.pdf

Hughes, J. and Donnelly, C. (2001) *Integrate or Segregate? Ten Years of Social Attitudes to Community Relations in Northern Ireland.* ARK Research Update 9, Belfast: ARK, Accessed Sept. 2013 at: www.ark.ac.uk/publications/updates/update9.pdf

Hughes, J. and Donnelly, C. (2003) *Attitudes to Community Relations in Northern Ireland: Grounds for Optimism?* ARK Research Update 20, Belfast: ARK, Accessed Sept. 2013 at: www.ark.ac.uk/publications/updates/update20.pdf

Leonard, M. and McKnight, M. (2011) Bringing Down the Walls: Young People's Perspectives on Peace Walls in Belfast. *International Journal of Sociology and Social Policy,* 31: 9/10, 569–82.

Lloyd, K. (2013) *Shared Education: Views of Children and Young People.* ARK Research Update 82, Belfast: ARK. Accessed Sept. 2013 at: www.ark.ac.uk/publications/updates/update82.pdf

MacGinty, R. (2003) *What Our Politicians Should Know.* ARK Research Update 18, Belfast: ARK. Accessed Sept. 2013 at: www.ark.ac.uk/publications/updates/update18.pdf

MacGinty, R. (2004) *Good Bargains?* ARK Research Update 29, Belfast: ARK. Accessed Sept. 2013 at: www.ark.ac.uk/publications/updates/update29.pdf

McEvoy, S. (2000) Communities and Peace: Catholic Youth in Northern Ireland. *Journal of Peace Research,* 37, 85–105.

Morrow, D. (2008) Shared or Scared? Attitudes to Community Relations Among Young People 2003–7. in: Schubotz, D. and Devine, P. (Eds.) *Young People in Post-Conflict Northern Ireland. The Past Cannot Be Changed, But The Future Can Be Developed.* Lyme Regis: Russell House Publishing.

Muldoon, O. et al. (2008) *Beyond Gross Divisions: National and Religious Identity Combinations in Northern Ireland.* ARK Research Update 58, Belfast: ARK. Accessed Sept. 2013 at: www.ark.ac.uk/publications/updates/update28.pdf

NICCY (2013) *Shared Education: The Views of Children and Young People.* Belfast: Northern Ireland Commissioner for Children and Young People.

NIO (Northern Ireland Office) (1998) *The Agreement, Text of the Agreement Reached in the Multi-Party Negotiations on Northern Ireland* (10 April 1998), (Cmnd. 3883) [Good Friday Agreement; Belfast Agreement]. Belfast: HMSO.

Nolan, P. (2012) *The Northern Ireland Peace Monitoring Report: Number One.* Belfast: Northern Ireland Community Relations Council.

Nolan, P. (2013) *The Northern Ireland Peace Monitoring Report: Number Two.* Belfast: Northern Ireland Community Relations Council.

OFMDFM (Office of the First Minister and Deputy First Minister) (2005) *A Shared Future: Improving Relations in Northern Ireland.* Belfast: OFMDFM.

OFMDFM (2010) *Programme for Cohesion, Sharing and Integration, Consultation Document.* Belfast: OFMDFM.

OFMDFM (2013) *Together: Building a United Community.* Belfast: OFMDFM.

Schubotz, D. and Devine, P. (2005) What Now? Exploring Community Relations Among 16-Year Olds in Northern Ireland. *Shared Space: A Research Journal on Peace, Conflict and Community Relations in Northern Ireland,* 1, 53–70.

Schubotz, D. and McCartan, C. et al. (2008) *Cross-Community Schemes: Participation, Motivation, Mandate, Final Project Report.* Belfast: ARK. Accessed Sept. 2013 at: www.ark.ac.uk/publications/occasional/crosscommunityschemesfinal.pdf

Schubotz, D. and Robinson, G. (2006) *Cross-Community Integration and Mixing: Does it Make a Difference?* ARK Research Update 43, Belfast: ARK. Accessed Sept. 2013 at: www.ark.ac.uk/publications/updates/update43.pdf

Smyth, M. et al. (2004) *The Impact of Political Conflict on Children in Northern Ireland.* Belfast: Institute for Conflict Research.

Todd, J. (2009) Northern Ireland: A Multi-phased History of Conflict to a Multi-levelled Process of Settlement. *Nationalism and Ethnic Politics,* 15: 3–4, 336–54.

CHAPTER 2

Rights and Democratic Participation: A Review of Evidence From YLT 1998 to 2012

Katrina Lloyd and Dirk Schubotz

Introduction

The rights of children and young people have always been at the forefront of ARK's work. The Young Life and Times (YLT) survey was initiated because it was felt that 'all too often the opinions of young people are ignored when decisions are made about many of the issues involving them.' The survey was seen as a potential platform that 'gives young people the chance to tell us about their experiences of school, and their views on politics, sectarianism and other social issues' (www.ark.ac.uk/ylt/about/). In fact, the very first YLT survey – which ran in 1998 as part of the Northern Ireland Life and Times (NILT) survey – included a module of questions which asked children and young people between the ages of 12 and 17 years about their rights.

In that first YLT survey, 43 per cent of respondents felt that that their views should be taken into account more, whilst just over half felt that the extent to which their views were taken into account was about right. Eighty per cent of this first cohort of YLT respondents also thought that their views mattered more than they had 20 years before. The same proportion of respondents (80%) agreed or strongly agreed that schools encourage teenagers to express their views, and 42 per cent said that their school had a school council. The final question that respondents to the first YLT survey were asked was whether they felt that it was *useful to have a regular survey like this of young people's views,* to which three quarters responded in the affirmative.

Whilst the methodology of the YLT survey has changed over the years (see the *Appendix* for details) YLT is now the longest established annual cross-sectional attitude survey of young people in the UK and Ireland. The issue of children's and young people's rights has been revisited by YLT in different contexts on a regular basis over these years, and a retrospective look at the data allows us to track changes with regard to young people's awareness of their rights in Northern Ireland. In this chapter, for the first time, we discuss how young people from diverse backgrounds differ in their knowledge of their rights. In particular, we look at how knowledge of rights varies among 16 year olds depending on gender, religion and the type of school they attend and at the ways in which pupils are provided with opportunities to participate in decision-making in their schools. Finally, we explore whether, and how, democratic participation in school is related to children's rights.

Knowledge about children's rights legislation

The right of children and young people to be consulted in matters that affect them is enshrined in the United Nation's Convention on the Rights of the Child (UNCRC) (UN, 1989) which was signed by the UK government in 1990, ratified in 1991, and which came into force in the UK in January 1992. One of the articles most frequently quoted with regard to children's rights and participation is Article 12, which states that:

> *States Parties shall assure to the child who is capable of forming his or her own views the right to express those views freely in all matters affecting the child, the views of the child being given due weight in accordance with the age and maturity of the child.*

(ibid)

In the second paragraph of Article 12, the UNCRC stipulates that 'the child shall in particular be provided the opportunity to be heard' in any judicial and administrative proceedings affecting the child.

The extent to which the rights of children and young people as set out in the Convention are implemented and upheld is investigated by UNICEF on a regular basis. UNICEF produces *General Comments* on particular Articles in the Convention (see O'Loughlin's discussion of the General Comment on Article 31 on Play in Chapter 5 of this book) and periodically requests specific monitoring reports from all governments that have ratified the Convention. In these reports, governments must report on the implementation of the Convention, whilst non-governmental organisations can also submit evidence. The UN Committee then issues its *Concluding Observations*, which highlight positive developments as well as gaps in the implementation of the UNCRC. In its last report, the UN Committee commented that the UK should 'take further steps to promote, facilitate and monitor systematic, meaningful and effective participation of all groups of children in society, including in schools, for example through school councils' (CRC/C/GBR/4, 2007: 33). The next UK government report to the UN Committee is scheduled for early 2014.

In Northern Ireland, the legal framework for the participation of children and young people is set by the *Ten-Year Strategy for Children and Young People in Northern Ireland*, which promises to create 'a culture where the views of our children and young people are routinely sought in matters which impact on their lives' (OFMDFM, 2006: 13). Several measures have been undertaken by government over the years to ensure compliance with international children's law and foster an environment in which children's and young people's views are routinely sought in matters that affect them. Arguably, the most important step was the establishment of the Office of the Northern Ireland Commissioner for Children and Young People (NICCY) in 2003. NICCY's main role is precisely the protection and promotion of children's rights in Northern Ireland, and it is no coincidence that one of the first activities undertaken by NICCY was to commission a report on children's rights in Northern Ireland (Kilkelly et al., 2004). This was followed by a review of rights in 2008 – *Children's Rights: Rhetoric or Reality? A Review of Children's Rights in Northern Ireland 2007/08*. The latter identified a range of *priority action areas*, which included 'the full incorporation of the UNCRC into domestic legislation to enable invocation of the Convention rights within national courts' (NICCY, 2008: 66).

In their book, *Theorizing Childhood*, James, Jenks and Prout (1998) describe how adults construct childhood and assign different levels of competency to children depending on the stage of development they feel children have reached. These perceived competencies are crucial in explaining why the incorporation of children's rights legislation can be slow and why there is reluctance among some adults to consult with children and young people. The authors differentiate between four levels of competency:

(a) *'the developing child'* – at which stage children are seen as incomplete adults and incompetent compared to adults.
(b) *'the tribal child'* – at this stage children are seen as highly competent within their own childhood culture, though not experts on adult life.
(c) *'the social child'* – in this phase children are perceived to have different but not necessarily inferior social competencies, communicating in different ways about similar issues to adults.
(d) *'the adult child'* – this is the phase in which children are seen as socially competent in ways comparable to adults.

Arguably, it is these *'adult children'* that are most likely to be involved in consultations with adults, possibly because adults believe it is easier to engage with older, rather than younger, children. This chapter examines whether the

YLT survey results can identify which children and young people have the greatest knowledge of their rights and are most likely to be consulted. It also examines the experiences of the children and young people themselves.

Awareness of the UNCRC

The first YLT survey in 1998 asked children and young people between the ages of 12 and 17 years about their knowledge of the UNCRC. In that year, 25 per cent of the 425 respondents to YLT said they had heard of the Convention (ARK, 1999). The question was repeated nine years later in the 2007 YLT survey, which by then had become a postal survey of 16 year olds run independently of NILT. In that year, 28 per cent of young people had heard of the UNCRC – an increase of only three percentage points compared to nine years earlier. Fast forwarding to the 2012 YLT, the figure for knowledge of the UNCRC among 16 year olds now sits at 40 per cent. Therefore, within the five-year period between 2007 and 2012, there has been a 12 percentage point rise in knowledge of the UNCRC.

Given the requirement of Article 42 of the UNCRC that governments should make the Convention known to all parents and children and, reflecting this, the efforts made by NICCY to raise awareness of children's rights among all citizens of Northern Ireland, it is somewhat encouraging that knowledge of the Convention is increasing, albeit slowly, among young people. However, the fact that six out of ten 16 year olds in Northern Ireland responding to the 2012 YLT survey said they were not aware of the UNCRC suggests there is still much to be done (Table 2.1).

Awareness levels of the UNCRC in Northern Ireland are similar to those in

Table 2.1 Respondents who had heard of the UNCRC, by year of survey

	%				
	Year of YLT survey				
Heard of the UNCRC?	1998*	2007	2009	2010	2012
Yes	25	28	33	39	40
No	72	70	62	57	60
Don't know	4	2	4	3	–

Source: 1998–2012 YLT surveys
*Respondents to 1998 YLT survey were aged between 12 and 17 years.

Scotland, but much higher than in England and Wales. The *UK Children's Commissioners' Report to UN Committee on the Rights of the Child* (2008: 9) noted that:

> *A survey in Scotland in 2007 found that 44% of children had heard of the UNCRC (ranging from some who knew a great deal about the Convention to some who had heard of it but who knew hardly anything about it). In England in 2006, a poll found that 13% of children had heard of the UNCRC. Even more startling, a recent survey found only 8% of Welsh children had heard of the Convention.*

Within Northern Ireland, while the YLT survey shows that knowledge of the UNCRC has been increasing among *all* 16 year old respondents to YLT over the years, one consistent finding has been that Catholics are more aware of the Convention than Protestants. For example, in 2007, 34 per cent of Catholics compared with 22 per cent of Protestants had heard of the UNCRC. By 2012, the figure for Catholic respondents was 45 per cent compared with 35 per cent for Protestants. Furthermore, in the YLT surveys from 2007 to 2012, young people who described themselves as Irish (the majority of whom were Catholic) were more likely to have heard of the UNCRC than those who described themselves as British (the majority of whom were Protestant). The figures for 2012 are presented in Table 2.2. Reflecting these findings, in the 2012 YLT survey, more young people who attended schools with all or mostly all Catholic pupils said they were aware of the UNCRC (46%) than those who attended schools with all or mostly all Protestant pupils (37%) or those who described their school as 'about half Catholic and half Protestant' (34%).

Respondents who attended academically selective grammar schools (44%) were more likely to say that they knew about the UNCRC than those from secondary (35%) or planned integrated schools (35%). Reflecting the findings outlined above, among grammar school pupils, those from a Catholic background were significantly more likely to say they knew about the UNCRC (47%) than those from a Protestant background (36%). Taken together, these data indicate that knowledge of the UNCRC is highest among well-educated Catholic adolescents responding to the YLT surveys.

Awareness of rights in general

While it is useful to know how many respondents to YLT are aware of the UNCRC, and to track this over time, it is equally important to assess the extent to which these young people actually know about the rights that are enshrined within the Convention. To address this, the 2007 and 2009 YLT surveys asked

Table 2.2 Characteristics of respondents who had heard of the UNCRC

	% of respondents who had heard of the UNCRC
Religion	
Catholic	45
Protestant	35
Identity	
British	35
Irish	47
Northern Irish	38
Ulster	25
Description of school	
All or mostly all Protestant	37
All or mostly Catholic	46
About half Protestant and half Catholic	34
Type of school	
Grammar	44
Secondary	35
Planned integrated	35

Source: 2012 YLT survey

respondents what they knew about the rights of children and young people living in Northern Ireland. Six per cent of respondents thought they did not have any rights at all (2007) and this figure had fallen to three per cent by 2009. It is somewhat encouraging that the percentage who thought they had rights and who said they could list a few had increased from 41 per cent in 2007 to 51 per cent in 2009 (Table 2.3).

While there was some slight variation in attitudes between religious groups, perceived religious mix of school and national identity, none of the differences were statistically significant. This would suggest that whilst young people from Protestant backgrounds may not associate the UNCRC with young people's rights, they may appear to have a similar level of awareness of their rights overall as their Catholic counterparts.

Knowledge of rights among younger children in Northern Ireland

In addition to running the YLT survey, in 2008 ARK developed the Kids' Life and Times (KLT) survey which is an annual survey of children aged 10 or 11

28 *Not So Different*

Table 2.3 Which statement below best describes what you know about the rights of children and young people living in Northern Ireland? (%)

	2007	2009
We don't have rights	6	3
We have rights, but I don't know anything about them	49	40
We have rights, and I could list a few	41	51
We have rights, and I know a great deal about them	4	6

Source: 2007 and 2009 YLT surveys

years who are in the final year of their primary education. Each year, approximately 4,000 children take part in the KLT survey. KLT has a different methodology to YLT; it is an online survey carried out in school. However, in some years, the same questions are asked in both surveys in order to gauge whether there are any differences in attitudes between the older and younger children, although occasionally the wording of the questions has to be changed to reflect the different age groups of the participants. In 2010 and 2012 questions on children's rights were asked in both YLT and KLT, and this provides an opportunity to compare the knowledge of rights of those at the end of their primary school with those at age 16. The data from the two surveys shows that fewer of the younger children participating in KLT in 2010 (25%) and 2012 (28%) had heard of the UNCRC compared to their 16 year old YLT counterparts (39% and 40% respectively) although a similar percentage in both age groups said they did not have any rights at all (4% KLT and 3% YLT).

In 2012, respondents to YLT and KLT were asked a series of questions relating to rights, some of which were clearly not rights that are enshrined within the UNCRC. Table 2.4 highlights that 10–11 year olds were much less aware of the rights they have compared to the 16 year old YLT respondents. As Table 2.4 shows, the majority of both YLT and KLT respondents said they had the right to a safe place to play although slightly more of the former (75%) were aware of this right than the latter (67%). The vast majority of children and young people recognised that they did not have the right to money to do the things they wanted or to decide whether they could go to school or not. Many more of the YLT respondents than the KLT respondents said they had the right to have their views listened to and taken seriously (88% and 59% respectively) and to have the right to an education (94% and 53% respectively). These findings suggest that while awareness-raising campaigns should be targeted at all children and young people in Northern Ireland, particular

Table 2.4 Perception of rights among primary year 7 children (KLT) and 16 year olds (YLT)

We have the right to ...	%	
	YLT	KLT
... have a safe place to play	75	67
... get more than £2 pocket money every week (KLT)	20	15
... have money to do the things we want (YLT)		
... have our ideas listened to and taken seriously	88	59
... have enough to eat (KLT)	86	50
... have enough food to survive (YLT)		
... decide to go to school or not (KLT)	8	10
... an education	94	53

Source: 2012 YLT and KLT surveys

emphasis should be placed on ensuring that younger children are made aware of the UNCRC and the rights that are enshrined within it.

Awareness of the Children's Commissioner among YLT respondents

The Children's Commissioners in all parts of the UK have the prime responsibility to safeguard the rights and best interests of children and young people. Modules on children's rights in the YLT surveys therefore contained questions asking about awareness of the Children's Commissioner and of NICCY's responsibilities. Among respondents to the 2012 YLT survey, 30 per cent said they did not know what the Commissioner does. Nearly half of all respondents (47%) had heard of NICCY; females were much more likely to say they had heard of NICCY than males (53% and 39% respectively). Since it is unlikely that females were particularly targeted by NICCY in awareness raising activities, this suggests that young women are either more interested in, or concerned about, the work of the Children's Commissioner, or alternatively that these activities should be more focused on young men.

Reflecting the increased knowledge of the UNCRC reported earlier among YLT respondents attending grammar schools in Northern Ireland, more of these young people were also aware of the Children's Commissioner and NICCY than their peers attending secondary or planned integrated schools. Just over half (53%) of grammar school pupils had heard of NICCY compared with 46 per cent of those attending planned integrated schools and just 41 per cent of secondary school pupils. Similarly, pupils attending grammar schools were most likely to have heard of the Children's Commissioner (37%) followed by those attending planned integrated schools (35%). Once again, pupils attending secondary schools were least likely to have heard of the Children's Commissioner (31%). Furthermore, higher proportions of YLT respondents attending grammar schools (73%) and planned integrated schools (74%) than attending secondary schools (66%) were aware that the Commissioner's job was to protect and promote the rights of children and young people. However, there was no evidence of the religious divide that existed with regard to awareness of the UNCRC. Equal proportions of Catholics (46%) and Protestants (45%) had heard of NICCY.

Education about equality, diversity and rights

The data presented so far in this chapter clearly shows that the type of school attended by young people is related to the extent of knowledge that young people have about their rights, including knowledge about the legal framework such as the UNCRC. Lundy (2006: 357) analyses in detail the impact and the paradoxes that a segregated education system can have on children's rights in a society coming out of conflict. She writes: 'Education, in particular, provides a good example of an area where civic society has been able to engage with human rights discourse and to harness the potential of the democratic processes to effect change'.

One such initiative in Northern Ireland is the Community Relations, Equality and Diversity Education (CRED) programme, which was set up to raise awareness of diversity in Northern Ireland's post-conflict society. Schools now have the statutory duty to teach young people about equality issues, respect and civil rights among people of different backgrounds (e.g. able-bodied and disabled, male and female, people of different ethnic backgrounds, sexual orientations, religious backgrounds etc.). How much of this is actually being taught will very much depend on individual schools and some diversity and equality issues are likely to be addressed more than others. For example, a school's 'ethos' may mean that teachers are afraid to, or not allowed to, talk to their pupils about sexual orientation, whilst gender equality issues or equality between people with and without disabilities are much less contentious and therefore may be much more likely to be addressed (Devine, 2013). Perhaps unsurprisingly, Devine noted that issues relating to equality between people of different religious or political persuasions were those that were most likely to be discussed in schools in Northern Ireland. Devine showed that around three quarters of the YLT respondents who had received CRED education, either in school or in a youth setting, did feel that this had given them more positive views towards all CRED groups.

What is most interesting here perhaps is that young people who said their school encouraged understanding of particular groups in society and promoted the equal treatment of different groups (via the CRED education programme) also had a better knowledge of the UNCRC than those whose school did not (44% and 34% respectively). Taken together with previous results reported in this chapter, these findings indicate that awareness of the UNCRC is related to religious background, national identity, attendance at particular schools in Northern Ireland, and participation and diversity programmes.

Perceptions on the role of government in protecting rights

Whilst awareness of rights is an important issue, it is perhaps equally meaningful to examine whether young people feel that the government, in practice, actually protects the rights of children and young people. The 2007 and 2009 YLT surveys asked respondents how well they thought the government protected their rights. In both years, only around eight per cent of young people thought the government protected their rights *'very well'* (Figure

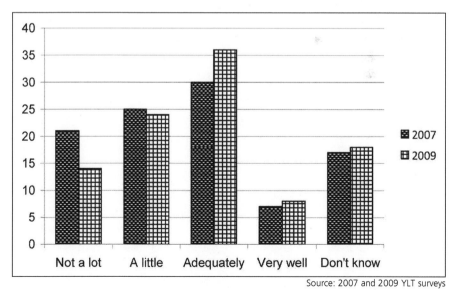

Source: 2007 and 2009 YLT surveys

Figure 2.1　Perception of how well the government protects the rights of young people (%)

2.1). Once again, while there was some variation in attitudes between religious groups, perceived religious mix of school and national identity, none of these differences were statistically significant.

In addition to asking about perceptions of how well the government protects their rights, respondents to YLT have also been asked, more generally, about their satisfaction with the way the Northern Ireland government does its job. Reflecting the findings in relation to the protection of their rights, in 2010, only 12 per cent of YLT respondents said they were 'very satisfied' or 'satisfied' with how the Northern Ireland government is doing its job. Nearly one third (32%) of respondents said they were 'dissatisfied' or 'very dissatisfied', whilst four in ten 16 year olds were 'neither satisfied nor dissatisfied'. Satisfaction with how the government was doing its job was higher among Protestants (15%) than Catholics (10%) and higher among males (16%) than females (10%). More males (33%) than females (21%) also thought things had improved for children and young people with the devolution of powers to the Stormont Government, although there was no difference in the views of Catholics and Protestants. Overall, 25% of respondents to the 2010 YLT survey thought the effect of the Stormont government on children and young people in Northern Ireland had been positive; the question was repeated in 2011 and in that year, nearly one third (31%) of respondents said things had improved for children and young people 'a little' or 'a lot'.

Every-day experiences of participation and rights

As noted, while it is important that children and young people know about the UNCRC and that they are valued by their government, it is equally important that they feel respected and valued by the adults with whom they share their lives (Ewan Nixon reflects on this in Chapter 8 of this book from the perspective of a 16 year old). Statistical evidence from the YLT surveys suggests that, in fact, the perception of the majority of young people in Northern Ireland is that they are judged negatively and treated with disrespect by adults because of their age. Eighty-three per cent of respondents to the 2010 YLT survey said they were judged negatively because they were young and 77 per cent said young people were portrayed 'mostly negatively' by the media. Two thirds of 16 year olds had experiences of being treated with suspicion in shops and nearly six in ten (57%) young people said they have been 'told to move on' when they have been standing with their friends in the street. O'Loughlin contextualises this latter finding in relation to young people's right to play in Chapter 5 of this book.

Experiences of being treated negatively were reported by the majority of 16 year olds and, overall, there was little difference in relation to variables such as gender and family financial background; however, those from Catholic backgrounds were much more likely than their Protestant peers (59% and 48% respectively) to say they had been told to move on in the street while young people who said their families were 'not well off' were much more likely than those who said their families were 'well off' to believe they had been treated as suspicious by staff in a shop or to have been told to move on in the street. In response to the question of how this made them feel, many 16 year olds expressed how '*angry and upset*' they felt because they had '*not done anything wrong*'. One 16 year old responded: 'Undermined as if I was some sort of human pollution littering the street. I felt rejected from society to a certain degree; lost my hope in the vision of equality in human treatment.'

A detailed analysis of these data was undertaken by NICCY (2011). The Commissioner's Office related these findings to the then latest UNCRC response to the UK Government report on the implementation of the UNCRC in 2008, which recommended that:

> . . . *the State party ensure full protection against discrimination on any grounds, including by taking urgent measures to address the intolerance and inappropriate characterisation of children, especially adolescents, within the society, including in the media* . . .

> (NICCY, 2011: 1)

This statement makes it clear that the UN Committee sees the negativity towards young people in society as an infringement of their rights, a view shared by McAlister, Scraton and Haydon (2009: 35) who noted in their report *Childhood in Transition: Experiencing Marginalisation and Conflict in Northern Ireland*, that 'adults generally considered young people to be anti-social and intimidating – young people were rarely viewed positively'.

Participation and say in school

So far, this chapter has portrayed a somewhat mixed picture. Whilst we noted some progress at the start of the chapter with regard to young people's awareness of their rights, in the previous section we also reported how the negativity that young people experience from adults in their community, in public places and in the media has a deleterious effect on them and can be seen as a violation of their right to be treated equally. In this section we examine the positive effects that participation in school and in the community can have for young people. Giving them an opportunity to participate in decision making, for example in school, can be seen as an implementation of their right to be consulted in matters that affect them, and the UNICEF's Rights-respecting Schools Award acknowledges schools that put the UNCRC at the heart of school life.

As reported in the introduction to this chapter, the very first YLT survey in 1998 found that around four in ten 12 to 17 year olds said that their school had a school council. Back then, 46 per cent of respondents said they had some say about the facilities in their school; one in five had some say on their uniforms, but influence on the curriculum and on the school's detention policy was much lower – around one in ten young people had some say in this. Eight years later, only 12 per cent of 16 year olds who responded to the 2006 YLT survey said they were allowed to express their views about the running of their school *a lot*. Whilst nearly six in ten (58%) respondents felt they could still express their views *a little*, over one quarter of 16 year olds said they could not express their views *at all* about the way their school is run. By that year the proportion of YLT respondents who had a council in their school had risen to 57 per cent, but only just over half (53%) of these respondents felt that their school council was effective (Sinclair, 2008). The matters in which young people had a say in each of the three main school sectors in Northern Ireland are presented in Table 2.5 which shows that it is still the case that only a minority of 16 year olds has a say in school-related matters, such as facilities and policies or uniform.

Table 2.5   Matters in school that respondents have a say about, by school type attended

	%			
	Grammar	Secondary	Integrated	All
School uniform	18	26	49	24
The budget	6	8	5	7
The curriculum	7	10	14	9
Facilities	42	42	54	43
School policies	36	49	67	44
Other	30	22	33	27

Source: 2006 YLT survey

Conclusions

In his commentary on children's rights, following analysis of data from the very first YLT survey in 1998, O'Halloran (2002: 143) argued that 'for any minority group to become genuinely empowered they must first know their rights and how they can be asserted'. He noted that the level of awareness among the young respondents to YLT was low at 25 per cent and he concluded that improvement was 'urgently required' (p. 154). Since then, there have been a number of important legal advances made in relation to children's rights in Northern Ireland, including the establishment of the Children's Commissioner. As the data presented in this chapter has shown, it is somewhat encouraging that knowledge of the Convention is increasing, albeit slowly, among young people. However, the fact that six out of ten 16 year olds in Northern Ireland responding to the 2012 YLT survey said they were not aware of the UNCRC suggests there is still much to be done, particularly in relation to young people from a Protestant community background and young people attending non-grammar schools. It is somewhat more encouraging that the percentage of YLT respondents who thought they had rights and who said they could list a few had increased from 41 per cent in 2007 to 51 per cent in 2009.

While contemporary law now recognises that children have rights to be asserted by them or by adults on their behalf (O'Halloran, 2002) nonetheless, research evidence is beginning to suggest that there may be another compelling reason why it is important for the younger generation to know about these rights, one which, according to UNICEF (2012: 23) 'opens an interesting field of study'. This relates to the recent finding by UNICEF that children who say they have been told about children's rights, or who have heard of the UNCRC, have higher levels of subjective wellbeing. This finding supports results from the 2007 YLT which showed that young people's wellbeing is very closely related to their rights and democratic participation in society. The survey found that those who were involved in decision making in their schools were happier in school and subsequently achieved better results (Schubotz, Simpson and Tennant, 2007). Taken together, these two sets of results suggest that increasing the awareness of their rights among children and young people may confer real benefits to their lives and is a finding that certainly merits further research.

References

ARK (1999) *Young Life and Times Survey [computer file] 1998*. ARK www.ark.ac.uk/ylt [distributor], June 1999. [Accessed Sept. 2013]

ARK (2013) *Kids Life and Times Survey* [computer file] 2013. ARK. www.ark.ac.uk/klt [distributor] [Accessed Sept. 2013]

CRC/C/GBR/4 (2007) *Committee on the Rights of the Child. Consideration of reports submitted by states parties under article 44 of the Convention. Third and fourth periodic reports of States parties due in 2007. United Kingdom of Great Britain and Northern Ireland UNCRC*. Accessed Sept. 2013 at: www2.ohchr.org/english/bodies/crc/crcs49.htm

Convention on the Rights of the Child (UNCRC) (2013) *The Right of the Child to Rest, Leisure, Play, Recreational Activities, Cultural Life and The Arts (Article 31)*. General Comment No. 17. Geneva: United Nations Office of the High Commissioner for Human Rights. Accessed Sept. 2013 at: www2.ohchr.org/english/bodies/crc/docs/GC/CRC-C-GC-17_en.doc

Devine, P. (2013) *Community Relations, Equality and Diversity in Education (CRED): Findings from the 2012 Young Life and Times Survey*. Belfast: ARK. Accessed 25 Sept. 2013 at: www.ark.ac.uk/publications/occasional/CREDYLT12.pdf

James, A., Jenks, C. and Prout, A. (1998) *Theorizing Childhood*. Cambridge: Polity Press.

Kilkelly, U. et al. (2004) *Children's Rights in Northern Ireland*. Belfast: NICCY.

Lundy, L. (2006) Mainstreaming Children's Rights in, to and Through Education in a Society Emerging from Conflict. *The International Journal of Children's Rights*, 14: 4, 339–62.

McAlister, S., Scraton, P. and Haydon, D. (2009) *Childhood in Transition: Experiencing Marginalisation and Conflict in Northern Ireland*. Belfast: Queen's University Belfast, Save the Children, Prince's Trust.

NICCY (Northern Ireland Commissioner for Children and Young People) (2008) *Children's Rights: Rhetoric or Reality? A Review of Children's Rights in Northern Ireland 2007/08*. Belfast: NICCY.

NICCY (2011) *Young People's Thoughts About and Experiences of Age-Related Negative Stereotyping An Analysis of Questions From the Young Life and Times Survey 2010*. Belfast: NICCY. Accessed Sept. 2013 at: www.niccy.org/uploaded_docs/2011/Publications/Findings%20of%20YLTS%202010%20negative%20stereotyping%20questions.pdf

OFMDFM (Office of the First Minister and Deputy First Minister) (2006) *Our Children – Our Pledge. A Ten-Year Strategy For Children and Young People in Northern Ireland 2006–2016*. Belfast: OFMDFM.

O'Halloran, K. (2002) The Rights of the Child in Northern Ireland: Teenage Attitudes and Social Responsibilities. In Gray, A. M., Lloyd, K., Devine, P., Robinson, G. and Heenan, D. (Eds.) *Social Attitudes in Northern Ireland: The Eighth Report*. London: Pluto Press.

Schubotz, D., Simpson, D. and Tennant, A. (2007) *Participation, Happiness and Achievement: The Impact of Poverty on The School Experiences of 16-Year Olds*. Belfast: Save the Children and ARK. Accessed Sept. 2013 at: www.ark.ac.uk/ylt/participation.pdf

Sinclair, R. (2008) Tackling Bullying in Schools: The Role of Pupil Participation. In Schubotz, D. and Devine, P. (Eds.) *Young People in Post-Conflict Northern Ireland. The Past Cannot Be Changed, But The Future Can Be Developed*. Lyme Regis: Russell House.

UK Children's Commissioners (2008) *UK Children's Commissioners' Report to UN Committee on the Rights of the Child*. London: UK Children's Commissioners. Accessed Sept. 2013 at www.childcomwales.org.uk/uploads/publications/61.pdf

UNICEF (2012) *Children's Well-Being From Their Own Point of View. What Affects The Children's Well-Being in The First Year of Compulsory Secondary Education in Spain?* Spain: UNICEF.

United Nations (1989) *United Nations Convention on the Rights of the Child*. Geneva: United Nations Office of the High Commissioner for Human Rights. Accessed 25 Sept. 2013 at: www.ohchr.org.

CHAPTER 3

Help Seeking and Support For Young People's Mental Health

Gavin Davidson

Background

Adolescence is often viewed as a complex, difficult and crucial time for the development of people's mental health and wellbeing. A shepherd in Shakespeare's *The Winter's Tale* proposes it is so difficult that it should be skipped altogether:

> *I would there were no age between ten and three-and-twenty, or that youth would sleep out the rest; for there is nothing in the between but getting wenches with child, wronging the ancientry, stealing, fighting.*
>
> (Act 3, Scene 3 as quoted in Patel et al., 2007)

Erikson (1972) suggested that for young people the key development task is to try to establish the many aspects of their identity which will form the rest of their lives. The research on the effects of trauma and adversity in these years reinforces the impact that experiences at this time may have throughout the life course for people's mental health, as well as across a range of other areas including their physical health, education, employment and risk of offending (Davidson, Devaney and Spratt, 2010). Although the complexities of adolescence are not new, there does seem to be increased concern about them; for example, a recent report by the Northern Ireland Association for Mental Health argued that:

> *In the past few years there has been a tremendous increase in the mental distress among our young people – depression and anxiety, self-harm, suicidal ideation and suicide. Other problems that we may not immediately connect with mental wellbeing, such as smoking, drug and alcohol misuse, teenage pregnancy, obesity and anti-social behaviour are associated with, and often exacerbated by low self-esteem and lack of emotional literacy. In NI and elsewhere, the suicide rates for young males aged 18–24 years have risen dramatically. The reasons remain unclear but it seems obvious that we are failing to provide future generations with the vital support they need in order to cope with the demands of modern life.*
>
> (Leavey et al., 2009: 19)

In this chapter, the findings from the Young Life and Times (YLT) survey will be presented within the relevant policy context and the international research literature on the prevalence, or level at any one time, of mental health problems among young people. The YLT findings are mainly from the 2008, 2009 and 2011 surveys, which included questions on mental health, general health and self-harm, and will concentrate on prevalence; responses to stress; and sources of support. In doing so, this chapter will also draw on previous analyses of mental health data from the YLT surveys (Schubotz, 2009, 2010) as well as discussing specific aspects of the findings in more depth and drawing conclusions with regard to implications for mental health policy and practice.

Although the YLT surveys currently provide the most comprehensive information available on the mental health of 16 year olds in Northern Ireland, it may still include some level of selection, response and non-response bias. Firstly, there is a possible under-estimate of prevalence due to the non-response of young people who are experiencing the most difficult mental health problems. For example, they may have been too unwell to complete the survey, or have been receiving hospital treatment. Secondly, findings from 16 year olds may not be generalisable to all children and young people as 16 year olds may experience specific stressors related to their psycho-social development such as increased exposure to alcohol and drugs; factors associated with intimate relationships; and other important transitional processes. Finally, whilst the survey provides very useful and interesting findings about associations between some factors, it cannot provide definite answers about the strength or direction of relationships between them, nor about the causality between two or more factors. For example, whilst the link between alcohol consumption and poor mental health is well known, it is not clear whether excessive drinking is caused by mental health problems or vice versa. Before considering the findings from the YLT surveys, however, the policy context in Northern Ireland is outlined. This context is important to examine as it provides some indication of the range of factors that need to be addressed to appropriately support young people's mental health.

Policy context

The overarching policy for children and young people in Northern Ireland is *Our Children and Young People – Our Pledge: A 10 Year Strategy for Children and Young People in Northern Ireland 2006–2016* (OFMDFM, 2006). Whilst it acknowledges the significance of 'growing awareness of the impact of "Troubles Related Trauma" on young people's mental health', it also concedes that 'the quality, consistency and accessibility of CAMH (Child and Adolescent Mental Health) services, is inadequate' (p. 30). The Strategy identified the need for more integrated children's services planning and the importance of increasing the focus on prevention and early intervention. It also specified the importance of coordinating developments across Departments, specifically with the policy framework for health promoting schools; mental health promotion; and the suicide prevention strategy. The 10 Year Strategy's call for a more integrated approach is being facilitated by the *Children and Young People's Strategic Partnership* (CYPSP) which was established in 2011, lead by the Health and Social Care Board, and produced the *Northern Ireland Children and Young People's Plan 2011–2014*. It has promoted outcomes-based planning; early intervention; family support hubs and greater integration in the commissioning and delivery of services.

The potential for schools to be a central aspect of addressing disadvantage has been set out in *Extended Schools: Schools, Families, Communities – Working Together* (DENI, 2006) and was reinforced in *Extended Schools – Building on Good Practice* (DENI, 2010: 1) which focuses on 'improving educational outcomes, reducing barriers to learning, and providing additional support to help improve the life chances of disadvantaged children and young people'. The regional family and parenting strategy *Families Matter: Supporting Families in Northern Ireland* (DHSSPS, 2009a) emphasised the benefits of prevention and early intervention, and set out how different levels of family support are intended to work towards families enjoying good physical and mental health and living a healthy lifestyle. The need for prevention and health promotion is further explored in *Healthy Child, Healthy Future. A Framework for the Universal Child Health Promotion Programme in Northern Ireland* (DHSSPS, 2010) which estimates that the prevalence of mental health problems amongst children and adolescents is currently at 20 per cent and states that 'mental health is a core component of all health professionals' work' (p. 20).

In response to the *Bamford Review of Mental Health and Learning Disability*, which was carried out in Northern Ireland between 2002 and 2007, the two Bamford Action Plans, 2009–2011 (DHSSPS, 2009b) and 2012–2014 (DHSSPS, 2012a), have continued to build on the direction of the *10-Year Strategy for Children and Young People*. Whilst the first Action Plan established early intervention work with children and young people as a priority, the more recent document set out plans to implement a stepped care model of CAMH services. This service model had been set out in more detail earlier in 2012

(DHSSPS, 2012b) and again emphasises the need for consideration of these issues across government and society:

> *Mental health and emotional wellbeing is everyone's business. It is not just the responsibility of professionals working in the field of child and adolescent mental health. It includes prevention, perinatal care, child development, child protection, physiological and family support, crisis resolution, community support and inpatient care.*

(p. 4)

Prevalence

In 2007, UNICEF – the *United Nations Children's Fund* – reported that, compared with 20 other developed countries, the United Kingdom (UK) had the worst record on children's well-being. A qualitative follow-up of this finding suggested that a range of factors may be involved, including families in the UK finding it more difficult to spend time together; to provide clear roles and rules; and to engage in outdoor and creative activities. It also highlighted the possible role of the relatively high levels of inequality and materialism identified in the UK (Nairn, 2011). In the most recent UNICEF report (2013) the UK is now 16th out of 29 countries, but still has the lowest rate of participation in further education for 15 to 19 year olds.

In Great Britain, based on two population-based samples of children and young people (importantly only those aged 5 to 15 and not including those in state care) in 1999 and 2004, Meltzer (2007) estimated that 9.5 per cent may be experiencing mental health problems at any one time. Collishaw et al. (2004) based on data collected in 1974, 1986 and 1999, found that there had been a substantial increase in conduct problems over that period, and that there was some evidence for a rise in emotional problems. The Department of Health (2011) in England has also estimated that, in any given year, 20 per cent of children and young people will have a mental health problem and about ten per cent at any one time.

In Northern Ireland, the *Bamford Review of Mental Health and Learning Disability* identified that most of the estimates of prevalence have been based on data from surveys conducted in Great Britain, and hypothesises that due to:

> *Northern Ireland's higher levels of socio-economic deprivation, ongoing civil strife and higher prevalence of psychological morbidity in the adult population . . . it is likely therefore that the prevalence of mental health problems and disorders in children and young people will be greater in NI than in other parts of the United Kingdom.*

(DHSSPS, 2006: 5)

Available evidence from Northern Ireland is inconclusive and suggests that there may be complexities in the comparisons with other countries. For example, Schubotz (2010: 45) reported that:

> *Prevalence of self-injury in Northern Ireland is similar to this of England (11%) and the Republic of Ireland (9%) found in the CASE study (Hawton and Rodham, 2006), but lower than this reported by O'Connor et al. (2009) for Scotland (14%).*

However, O'Connor et al. (2010) found that the prevalence of lifetime self-harm among Northern Irish adolescents was significantly lower than that reported in the Republic of Ireland, Scotland and England, and suggested that this may reflect a greater reluctance to disclose which may be related to the 'Troubles'. Several other authors also highlighted that the 'Troubles' have had an important additional impact on the mental health of children and young people in Northern Ireland through the negative impact on the socio-economic context and the high levels of trauma and loss which may extend across generations (Fay, Morrisey and Smyth, 1999; OFMDFM, 2002; O'Reilly and Stevenson, 2003; Ferry et al., 2008; Leavey et al., 2009; Macdonald et al., 2011).

Research that identified relatively high levels of self-harm and suicide in Northern Ireland suggested that trauma may be an important factor. Jordan et al. (2011) reported that there was a 64 per cent increase in suicide in Northern Ireland between 1999 and 2008, largely due to a rise in male suicide, particularly marked in the 15 to 34 year age group which accounted for 72 per cent of all male suicides in 2008.

Tomlinson (2007, 2012) has examined the suicide trends in Northern Ireland over the past 40 years. His studies show that 'the cohort of children and young people who grew up in the worst years of violence, during the 1970s, have the highest and most rapidly increasing suicide rates, and account for the steep upward trend in suicide following the 1998 Agreement.' (Tomlinson, 2012: 464).

Tomlinson concludes that contrary to Durkheim's view [who suggested that conflict reduces suicide through greater social integration]:

> *The recent rise in suicide involves a complex of social and psychological factors. These include the growth in social isolation, poor mental health arising from the experience of conflict, and the greater political stability of the past decade. The transition to peace means that externalised aggression is no longer socially approved. It becomes internalised instead.*

> (ibid: 464)

The *National Confidential Inquiry into Homicide and Suicide by People with Mental Illness* (2011) report on Northern Ireland also emphasised the possible associations with inequality, deprivation, substance misuse and self-harm. According to the report:

> *Young people who died by suicide were more likely than other age groups to be living in the poorest areas in Northern Ireland and had the lowest rate of contact with mental health services (15%). The young mental health patients who died by suicide tended to have high rates of drug misuse (65%), alcohol misuse (70%) and previous self-harming features (73%).*

(p. 18)

The Inquiry also highlighted that the largest difference between suicide rates in Northern Ireland and other United Kingdom countries was in young people (Devaney et al., 2012). More recently, the *All-Ireland Young Men and Suicide Project* (Richardson, Clarke and Fowler, 2013) explored the importance of the economic downturn and associated unemployment on young men's mental health.

To inform the ongoing debate about mental health and suicide in Northern Ireland, since 2004 the YLT survey has regularly included the GHQ-12, which is a 12-question version of the General Health Questionnaire (Goldberg, 1978; Goldberg and Huxley, 1980) to identify potential mental health problems. Two scoring systems allow the GHQ-12 data to be used in different ways. Firstly, a mean score can be calculated and compared across different respondent groups. Secondly, using a different scoring system, a 'caseness' threshold or score can also be used to indicate a possible mental health problem. Lloyd et al. (2008) discussed YLT survey findings on the GHQ-12 from the first five YLT survey years in detail, whilst, in Chapter 4 of this book, Shevlin and Murphy examine the relationship of loneliness and mental health, using the UCLA loneliness scale and the GHQ-12 questionnaire. An earlier analysis of this data by the authors suggested that loneliness is associated with poorer mental health, and the association appears to be stronger for females (Murphy and Shevlin, 2012).

In 2011, the most recent survey year to include the GHQ-12, the overall mean score was 11.4. Reflecting the pattern consistently found in previous research, the mean score for females was higher than that for males. Using the 'caseness' scoring method, the results show that more than a quarter (28%) of the young people who responded scored at a level which indicates a possible mental health problem. The figure for females was almost twice that for males (36% and 19% respectively).

Schubotz's (2010) detailed analysis of GHQ-12 results over time found an overall increase from 2004 to 2008. Young people from not-well-off

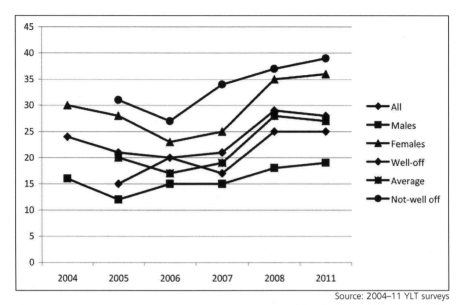

Source: 2004–11 YLT surveys

Figure 3.1   GHQ-12 'caseness', by survey year, sex and family financial background (%)

backgrounds were more likely to be a 'case' (37% compared to 25% from well-off backgrounds). He concluded that 'females from not-well-off backgrounds were more than twice as likely as males from well-off backgrounds to be GHQ "cases" (40% and 17% respectively)' (p. 16). Figure 3.1 includes the most recent data and indicates that this pattern is evident among the respondents to the 2011 survey.

The YLT survey results show that another group more likely to be affected by poor mental health are same-sex-attracted 16 year olds, who were also more likely to be bullied at school (McNamee, Lloyd and Schubotz, 2008). In the 2011 YLT survey, the GHQ-12 score for same-sex-attracted respondents was 15.1, compared to 11.2 for opposite-sex attracted, and this difference is statistically significant and consistent with earlier findings.

The 2011/12 Health Survey Northern Ireland (DHSSPS, 2012c) also included the GHQ-12 questionnaire. The survey found that 19 per cent of respondents (aged 16 or over) scored four or more on the GHQ-12 indicating a possible mental health problem. The rate among 16 to 24 year olds was 18 per cent.

The first *Subjective Well-being Annual Population Survey* was carried out within the UK in 2011 and 2012. This involved four key questions: life satisfaction; extent that things are worthwhile; happiness yesterday and anxiety yesterday. Within the *Northern Ireland Peace Monitoring Report*, Nolan (2013) has reported that based on this survey, people living in Northern Ireland enjoy a relatively good sense of well-being. 'The 16–19 and 65–79 age cohorts rated their life satisfaction highest. Northern Ireland scored higher than the UK average on all four questions' (p. 117). At the same time, however, Nolan notes that 'the number taking their own lives has risen from 159 in 2001 to 289 in 2012, which means that Northern Ireland has gone from having the lowest rate of suicide in the UK to the highest' (p. 118). These figures are a stark reminder of the complexities of experiencing, researching and responding to factors associated with mental health.

Responses to stress

Being 16 years of age brings with it many stresses and worries, as Ewan Nixon's reflections in his contribution to this book clearly show. Four out of five respondents to the 2008 YLT survey said that schoolwork and exams made them stressed, and other issues included family problems and issues relating to finances or work. However, it is the way that young people respond to these stresses and worries that can affect their mental health. Such responses can take many forms and YLT participants were asked how often they do any of a list of eight things (both positive and negative) when they are worried or upset. The vast majority said that they would sometimes or often *talk to someone* (98%) or *try to sort things out* (92%). At the same time, however, 89 per cent said that they would *get angry*. Figure 3.2 shows that the responses of males and females to being upset are quite different. Females are more likely than males to *get angry*, *talk to someone*, *blame themselves for getting into the mess*, or *stay in their room*. In contrast, males are more likely than females to *try to sort things out*. However, similar proportions of males and females said they would *try not to think about what is worrying them*. Coincidentally, these figures nearly match those saying that they would think about how they have dealt with such situations in the past.

The figures overall suggest that females have a wider range of responses than males, which reflects Harland's contention that 'by withholding certain feelings and emotions young men can believe they are expressing an important aspect of their masculinity' (2009: 6). However, for those male YLT respondents who only identified one regular response to worry, just over one half of them (54%) said that this was to *try to sort it out*.

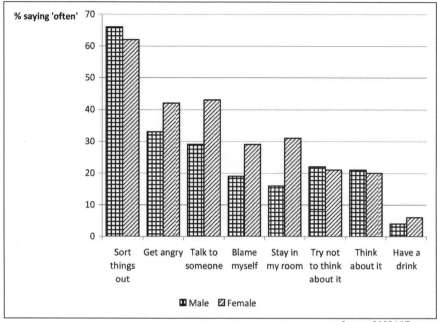

Source: 2008 YLT survey

Figure 3.2   Responses to worry, by sex

Self-harm

For some young people their response to stress and worry is to self-harm or take an overdose (which can be a form of self-harm or a suicide attempt). The suicide prevention strategy, *Protect Life* (DHSSPS, 2006) was further developed in 2012 (DHSSPS, 2012d) based on the available research, to focus more on addressing the needs of men aged 15 to 45 from deprived areas. It also proposed the greater use of information technology to engage younger people, and the potential negative and positive roles of social media do perhaps need to be explored further (McGorry, Bates and Birchwood, 2013). As Tomlinson (2012) reported, the number of suicides has increased since the suicide prevention strategy has been in place and, as the strategy acknowledges, attempts to prevent suicide require much wider efforts to address the range of societal issues involved.

In 2008, around one in seven YLT respondents (14%) said that they had seriously thought about taking an overdose or trying to harm themselves in the previous year, although they had not done it, with more females than males saying this (18% and 7% respectively). A distinct pattern is also evident in relation to family financial background, as less well-off respondents were more likely to have seriously considered taking an overdose (22%), when compared with average (11%) or well-off respondents (13%).

As we might expect, there are some differences in the responses to worry among those young people who had seriously considered harming themselves, compared to those who had not. In particular, the former group were more likely to say that they often *blame themselves for getting into a mess* (48% compared to 21%), *get angry* (61% compared to 35%) or *stay in their room* (47% compared to 22%). Conversely, this group is less likely to try to *sort things out* (35% compared to 68%).

Looking next at those who have taken an overdose or tried to harm themselves in some other way, around one in ten had done this (see Table 3.1). This figure was equally split between those who have done this once, and those who have done this more than once. This was more prevalent among females than males (13% compared with 5% respectively). Yet again, a pattern is evident in relation to family financial background, with less-well-off respondents (16%) being most likely to have taken an overdose or self-harmed compared with others. However, it is important to note that there is a higher proportion of females within the 'not-well-off' category than among participants overall, which may compound this pattern.

There was an association between self-harm and alcohol intake, with those who have drunk alcohol being much more likely to have considered self-harm (23%) than others. Furthermore, this group is also more likely to have self-harmed (17%). As well as the association with general alcohol use, those respondents who said that they drink alcohol as a specific response to stress or worry were more likely to have thought about self-harm compared to those

Table 3.1 'Have you ever deliberately taken an overdose?', by sex, and by family financial background

	%					
	Male	Female	Not-well-off	Average	Well-off	All
No	95	87	84	91	92	90
Yes, once	3	6	9	5	3	5
Yes, more than once	2	7	7	4	6	5

Source: 2008 YLT survey

who did not do this (25% and 9% respectively). However, the association between alcohol use and self-harm is less obvious.

There was also an association between having been bullied at school and thinking about self-harm (23%), compared to those who had not been bullied (8%). Furthermore, those who have been bullied at school were more likely to have taken an overdose or harmed themselves in some other way (18% compared to 6%).

However much these statistics tell us about responses to worry and self-harm, it is in the words of the 16 year olds themselves that we find the full complexity of feelings and responses. The following two quotes are examples of this:

> *A lot of young people who self-harm do it because they are down, depressed or are being bullied. This can make them mentally feel worthless and feel that there is no other way out. So, I think that there should be more done in school to show young people that there is a way out and that there are people to talk to.*

> *For many young people, we feel that no one would want us to stay here, and not many of our friends have experience on what to do in these cases. There are so many pressures on young adults, girls especially, that many of us feel that there is no way out, no escape other than to end the hurt . . . I feel that depression is something that is quite common and it's the people who keep it a secret that need the most help although not many people offer them a helping hand.*

Sources of support

The 2008 YLT survey asked about possible sources of support for young people who may be experiencing difficulties. Table 3.2 shows that the most likely source of support for young people were friends, with 90 per cent of respondents saying that they are able to talk to a friend about things that really bother them, followed by talking to their mothers (79%). The latter figure reinforces the importance of family in providing support for young people, a key feature of *Families Matter: Supporting Families*. This was confirmed by the 2009 YLT survey results which showed that respondents' friends and mothers are also regarded as the *most helpful* source when emotional or mental health problems arise (Schubotz, 2010). In contrast, however, given the role of schools highlighted in the *Healthy Child, Healthy Future* framework, teachers are least commonly cited, with just over one third of all respondents identifying these as source of support.

In contrast to the gender differences in responses to stress identified earlier in the chapter, there was less variation in the sources of support identified by

Table 3.2   In general, are you able to talk to the following people about things that really bother you?

	%		
	Male	Female	All
Your father	65	55	59
Your mother	77	80	79
A brother or sister	61	63	62
Another relative	53	58	56
A friend	86	93	90
A teacher	39	37	38
Somebody else	29	43	38

Source: 2008 YLT survey

young men and young women. The main exception was that young men were more likely than young women to say that they could talk to their father (with a ten-percentage point difference). Nevertheless, mothers were still identified as source of support by a higher proportion of young men than fathers were. The largest male/female difference related to *somebody else*, with more females identifying these. Around half of the different 'other' sources of support were the respondent's boyfriend or girlfriend, and this was particularly evident for female respondents. Youth workers/leaders accounted for nine per cent.

The mean number of sources of support identified by respondents was 3.8, with only two per cent of young people identifying none, whilst four per cent identified all seven sources. The pattern for males and females is very similar. Thus, most young people have access to several sources of support, with friends and mothers being the most available of these.

Parental interaction was explored further in the survey, and in general, relationships with fathers appear to be more harmonious than with mothers. Table 3.3, which only includes responses from those young people who have the relevant person in their lives, around one half of YLT participants said that they hardly ever quarrel with their father, whilst 38 per cent said this about their mother. Young men were more likely than young women to say that they hardly ever quarrel with a parent, and this is especially true in relation to arguing with their mother.

At the same time, however, a higher proportion of respondents said that they hardly ever talk to their father about things that matter to them, than talk

Table 3.3 Frequency of parental interaction

	%					
	Quarrel with your mother?			Talk to mother about things that matter?		
	All	Male	Female	All	Male	Female
Most days	9	8	10	37	27	44
More than once a week	24	18	28	19	23	17
Less than once a week	26	27	26	16	17	15
Hardly ever	38	43	34	24	29	21
Don't know	3	4	2	4	5	3
	Quarrel with your father?			Talk to father about things that matter?		
Most days	7	7	8	16	17	15
More than once a week	15	14	16	16	20	14
Less than once a week	25	25	24	19	18	19
Hardly ever	49	50	48	44	38	48
Don't know	4	4	4	5	6	4

Source: 2008 YLT survey

to their mother, and this was especially true for young women. This suggests that interaction with mothers (both positive and negative) is higher than for interaction with fathers, and reflects the findings of Devine and Lloyd (2004) using Wave 3 of the Northern Ireland Household Panel Survey.

Professional help

In Northern Ireland there are a range of services providing specialist mental health support for young people. These include therapeutic services provided through schools and social services; primary care; counselling and mental health organisations in the voluntary and community sector; and specialist CAMH Services. When asked if they had had any serious personal, emotional, behavioural or mental health problem for which they felt that they needed professional help (such as a GP, social worker, psychologist, psychiatrist or telephone helpline), three quarters of respondents in 2008 and in 2009 said that they had had few or no problems. A further seven per cent said that, whilst they had had serious problems, they had not felt the need for professional help. This means that one in five young people in each year said that they had had serious problems in the previous 12 months for which they felt that they needed professional help – with a slightly lower proportion of males (16%) compared with females (22%).

YLT respondents who had reported serious mental or emotional health problems over the past 12 months had more negative attitudes and experiences of mental health services than their counterparts (Schubotz, 2010). For example, just under one third (31%) of young people felt that there are very few services for young people who have emotional or mental health problems, and this was significantly higher among those who said that they have had such problems (45%) compared to those who had not (25%). The pattern of agreement was very similar in relation to the statement *'The voice of young people who have emotional or mental health problems is not heard by health professionals'* (45% and 27% respectively). The following quote from a 2009 YLT respondent represents some of the frequently raised concerns with regard to professional mental health services:

> *Depression, especially in young people, is not dealt with or picked up on quickly and efficiently enough. The government should invest more money in counselling in schools etc. to help young people particularly bereaved young people to cope with whatever they're going through.*

The Bamford Review's (2006: 2) report on CAMH services acknowledged that 'Mental health services for children in NI have received too little attention for too long and have suffered from a lack of coherent planning and investment'. It also engaged with some of the specific areas of need which aren't considered in depth in this chapter but are important to acknowledge. These include children and young people with learning disabilities; with autistic spectrum disorder (ASD); attention deficit hyperactivity disorder (ADHD); feeding and eating disorders; looked after children; children and young people who have experienced abuse; children and young people who misuse alcohol and substances; those in contact with the criminal justice system; lesbian, gay, bisexual and trans-gender people (LBGT) children and young people; and those from ethnic minorities.

Discussion and conclusion

An important issue from the YLT survey findings is that the survey identified an increase of 16 year olds who may have mental health problems from 20 per cent in 2006, to 29 and 28 per cent in 2008 and 2011 respectively. A more detailed analysis of the prevalence findings identified that 40 per cent of young women from not-well-off backgrounds met the threshold for possible mental health problems which reinforces the case for a more in-depth prevalence survey.

Alarmingly, as highlighted above, a commonly-used estimate of prevalence in Northern Ireland (9.5%) is based on the 1999 and 2004 samples from GB (Green et al., 2005; Meltzer, 2007) which only included 5 to 15 year olds, did not include looked after children and did not reflect the range of impacts of the Troubles. Based on this conservative estimation, the Bamford Review (2006) suggested that approximately 45,000 children and young people, aged 5 to 15, needed intervention from CAMH services. However, in the subsequent Bamford Action Plan (DHSSPS, 2009b) the important detail of this estimated figure was no longer specified and it was stated 'in Northern Ireland: 250,000 adults and 45,000 children and young people have a mental health need at any one time' (p. 15). Thus, in a review of the research priorities for the mental health of children and young people in Northern Ireland Macdonald et al. (2011) recommended that a prevalence study specific to Northern Ireland should be commissioned.

The findings on the support available to young people confirm that the vast majority do feel able to talk with someone, and most identified that they could talk with friends and/or family, especially their mother. These findings reinforce the importance of not only focusing on the individual young person's ability to manage their own mental health, but also of further developing more systemic approaches which facilitate family and peer support. The findings on relationships with parents and young people's responses to worry or stress further support the need to be facilitating the development of emotional health and well-being with the involvement of families. To address this, since 2007 the Department of Education has been leading on a very positive initiative to promote pupils' emotional health and wellbeing (Connolly et al., 2011).

In terms of professional support, over one quarter of 16 year olds identified that they had had a serious personal, emotional, behavioural or mental health problem, but only nine per cent sought professional help. Although professional help is not necessary for every serious problem, this would suggest there is unmet need for support and might raise issues about the level and accessibility of services. The associations with self-harm also provide information about the extent of this issue and how policy and services may respond. A key finding was that one in ten YLT respondents had tried to harm themselves, with five per cent having done this once, and five per cent more than once. As reported above, self-harming behaviour was more common among young women and those from not-well-off backgrounds. This provides clear direction both for the targeting of intervention and for the possible underlying factors which also need to be addressed.

Those who have used alcohol and been bullied were also more likely to have thought about self-harming or harmed themselves. There was a particularly strong association found between alcohol use when upset and self-harm. These findings may also inform the ongoing efforts to prevent suicide as, although self-harm does not necessarily indicate that the young person intends to take their own life, accidental death can be the result of self-harm, and those who self-harm are also more likely to intentionally take their own lives (Hawton and James, 2005). As Macdonald et al. (2011) concluded – and these findings reinforce this – there are groups who are at higher risk of self-harm and suicide and the issues involved are complex, involving developmental, individual, family, community and societal factors. Nock (2012) has recommended we need further research on how and why these known risk factors lead to self-harm; possible ways for better predicting self-harm; and the further evaluation of the range of prevention programmes that may be needed.

There are also a number of areas which may be useful to further explore in future YLT surveys. The impact of trauma and adversity on a range of issues could be examined by including the *Adverse Childhood Experiences* questionnaire (Felitti et al., 1998) which would also allow comparison across countries and groups. The role of social media in the lives of 16 year olds, including the impact on their mental health and wellbeing, would seem an emerging area that could be important to explore. Analysis of the Kids' Life and Times survey of 10/11 year olds found a negative relationship between psychological wellbeing and the frequency of use of social networking sites, especially among girls (Devine and Lloyd, 2012). Finally, in light of the findings on the importance of inequalities, it could be useful to explore young people's views of how society should be structured and what the priorities for social policy for 16 year olds should be.

To conclude, the mental health of young people is central to the effective social and economic functioning of any society now and in the future. In order to address young people's mental health it is essential to have an accurate picture of the extent of their needs. The clearest message from these results from the YLT survey is that there is an urgent need for a prevalence survey of the mental health of the children and young people of Northern Ireland of all ages and in all settings. The findings suggest that the estimates currently being used to develop and deliver services may be underestimating levels of need.

The findings also provide local data on the impact of inequalities, with perhaps the most striking being the difference in prevalence between young women from not well-off backgrounds and young men from well-off backgrounds. The international research on the importance of the level of inequalities in a society across a wide range of issues is extremely convincing (Wilkinson and Pickett, 2009) and it seems reasonable to emphasise that efforts to respond to these mental health problems at the individual level, without addressing the underlying societal issues, will not be as effective (Schubotz, 2010). Moreover, the findings on self-harm further reinforce the importance both of addressing inequality and of understanding how the complex issues and relationships involved may be related and interact.

References

Bamford Review of Mental Health and Learning (2006) *Child and Adolescent Mental Health Services: A Model Service*. Belfast: DHSSPS.

Collishaw, S., Maughan, B., Goodman, R. and Pickles, A. (2004) Time Trends in Adolescent Mental Health. *Journal of Child Psychology and Psychiatry*, 45: 8, 1350–627.

Connolly, P. et al. (2011) *Pupils' Emotional Health and Wellbeing: A Review of Audit Tools and a Survey of Practice in Northern Ireland Post-Primary Schools*. Belfast: Centre for Effective Education, Queen's University Belfast.

Davidson, G., Devaney, J. and Spratt, T. (2010) The Impact of Adversity in Childhood on Outcomes in Adulthood: Research Lessons and Limitations. *Journal of Social Work*, 10: 4, 369–90.

DENI (Department of Education) (2006) *Extended Schools: Schools, Families, Communities – Working Together*. Bangor: DENI.

DENI (2010) *Extended Schools – Building on Good Practice*. Bangor: DENI.

Department of Health (2011) *No Health Without Mental Health: A Cross-Government Mental Health Outcomes Strategy For People of All Ages, Analysis of the Impact on Equality (AIE), Annex B – Evidence Base*. London: DoH.

Devaney, J., Bunting, L., Davidson, G., Hayes, D., Lazenbatt, A. and Spratt, T. (2012) *Still Vulnerable The Impact of Early Childhood Experiences on Adolescent Suicide and Accidental Death*. Belfast: Northern Ireland Commissioner for Children and Young People.

Devine, P. and Lloyd, K. (2004) *Bringing up Baby*. ARK Research Update 40, Belfast: ARK. Accessed Sept. 2013 at: www.ark.ac.uk/publications/updates/update40.pdf

Devine, P. and Lloyd, K. (2012) Internet Use and Psychological Well-being Among 10-Year-Old and 11-Year-Old Children. *Child Care in Practice,* 18: 1, 1357–5279.

DHSSPS (Department of Health, Social Services and Public Safety) (2006) *Protect Life: A Shared Vision – The Northern Ireland Suicide Prevention Strategy and Action Plan 2006–2011*. Belfast: DHSSPS.

DHSSPS (2009a) *Families Matter: Supporting Families in Northern Ireland*. Belfast: DHSSPS.

DHSSPS (2009b) *Delivering the Bamford Vision: The Response of the Northern Ireland Executive to the Bamford Review of Mental Health and Learning Disability Action Plan 2009–2011*. Belfast: DHSSPS.

DHSSPS (2010) *Healthy Child, Healthy Future A Framework for the Universal Child Health Promotion Programme in Northern Ireland.* Belfast: DHSSPS.

DHSSPS (2012a) *Delivering the Bamford Vision: The Response of the Northern Ireland Executive to the Bamford Review of Mental Health and Learning Disability Action Plan 2012–2015.* Belfast: DHSSPS.

DHSSPS (2012b) *Child and Adolescent Mental Health Services: A Service Model.* Belfast: DHSSPS.

DHSSPS (2012c) *Health Survey Northern Ireland: First Results From The 2011/12 Survey.* Belfast: DHSSPS.

DHSSPS (2012d) *Protect Life: A Shared Vision – The Northern Ireland Suicide Prevention Strategy 2012-March 2014.* (Refreshed June 2012) Belfast: DHSSPS.

Erikson, E.H. (1972) *Childhood and Society.* Harmondsworth: Penguin Books.

Fay, M.T., Morrissey, M. and Smyth, M. (1999) *Northern Ireland's Troubles: The Human Costs.* London: Pluto Press.

Felitti, V.J. et al. (1998) Relationship of Adult Health Status to Childhood Abuse and Household Dysfunction to Many of the Leading Causes of Death in Adults. *American Journal of Preventive Medicine,* 14: 4, 245–58.

Ferry, F. et al. (2008) *Trauma, Health and Conflict in Northern Ireland: A Study of The Epidemiology of Trauma-Related Disorder and Qualitative Investigation of The Impact of Trauma on The Individual.* Omagh: The Northern Ireland Centre for Trauma and Transformation.

Goldberg, D. (1978) *Manual of the General Health Questionnaire.* Windsor: National Foundation for Educational Research.

Goldberg, D. and Huxley, P. (1980) *Mental Illness in the Community: The Pathway to Psychiatric Care.* London: Tavistock Publications.

Green, H. et al. (2005) *Mental Health of Children and Young People in Great Britain, 2004.* Basingstoke: Palgrave Macmillan.

Harland, K. (2009) *Key Issues in Promoting Mental Health: Masculinity and Mental Health. Paper written for the Design for Living Partnership.* Belfast: Action Mental Health, The Youth Council for Northern Ireland and The Health Promotion Agency NI.

Hawton, K. and James, A. (2005) Suicide and Deliberate Self-Harm in Young People. *British Medical Journal,* 330: 7496, 891–4.

Hawton, K. and Rodham, K. with Evans, E. (2006) *By Their Own Young Hand. Deliberate Self-Harm and Suicidal Ideas in Adolescents.* London: Jessica Kingsley.

Jordan, J., McKenna, H., Keeney, S. and Cutcliffe, J. (2011) *Providing Meaningful Care: Using Experiences of Young Suicidal Men to Inform Mental Health Care Services.* Belfast: Public Health Agency.

Leavey, G., Galway, K., Rondon, J. and Logan, G. (2009) *A Flourishing Society: Aspirations for Emotional Health and Wellbeing in Northern Ireland.* Belfast: Northern Ireland Association for Mental Health.

Lloyd, K., Cairns, E., Doherty, C. and Ellis, K. (2008) *Adolescent Mental Health in Northern Ireland: Empirical Evidence From The Young Life and Times Survey.* In Schubotz, D. and Devine, P. (Eds.) *Young People in Post-Conflict Northern Ireland. The Past Cannot Be Changed But The Future Can Be Developed.* Lyme Regis: Russell House Publishing.

Macdonald, G., Livingstone, N., Davidson, G., Sloan, S., Fargas, M. and McSherry, D. (2011) *Improving the Mental Health of Northern Ireland's Children and Young People: Priorities for Research.* Belfast: Public Health Agency and Queen's University Belfast.

McGorry, P., Bates, T. and Birchwood, M. (2013) Designing Youth Mental Health Services For The 21st Century: Examples From Australia, Ireland and the UK. *British Journal of Psychiatry, Supplement* 54: s30–5.

McNamee, H., Lloyd, K., Schubotz, D. (2008) Same Sex Attraction, Homophobic Bullying and Mental Health of Young People in Northern Ireland. *Journal of Youth Studies*, 11: 1, 33–46.

Meltzer, H. (2007) Childhood Mental Disorders in Great Britain: An Epidemiological Perspective. *Child Care in Practice*, 13: 4, 313–26.

Murphy, S. and Shevlin, M. (2012) *Loneliness in Northern Ireland Adolescents.* ARK Research Update 81, Belfast: ARK, Accessed Sept. 2013 at www.ark.ac.uk/publications/updates/update81.pdf

Nairn, A. (2011) *Children's Well-being in UK, Sweden and Spain: The Role of Inequality and Materialism. A Qualitative Study.* London: Ipsos Mori Social Research Institute.

National Confidential Inquiry into Suicide and Homicide by People with Mental Illness (2011) *Suicide and Homicide in Northern Ireland.* Manchester: University of Manchester.

Nock, M.K. (2012) Future Directions for the Study of Suicide and Self-Injury. *Journal of Clinical Child and Adolescent Psychology*, 41: 2, 255–9.

Nolan, P. (2013) *Northern Ireland Peace Monitoring Report Number Two.* Belfast: Northern Ireland Community Relations Council.

O'Connor, R.C., Rasmussen, S., Miles, J. and Hawton, K. (2009) Self-harm in Adolescents: Self-Report Survey in Schools in Scotland. *British Journal of Psychiatry*, 194: 1, 68–72.

O'Connor, R.C., Rasmussen, S. and Hawton, K. (2010) *Northern Ireland Lifestyle and Coping Survey: Final Report*, Belfast: DHSSPS.

OFMDFM (Office of the First Minister and Deputy First Minister) (2002) *Reshape, Rebuild, Achieve.* Belfast: OFMDFM.

OFMDFM (2006) *Our Children and Young People – Our Pledge: A 10 Year Strategy for Children and Young People in Northern Ireland 2006–2016.* Belfast: OFMDFM.

O'Reilly, D. and Stevenson, M. (2003) Mental Health in Northern Ireland: Have 'The Troubles' Made it Worse? *Journal of Epidemiology and Community Health*, 57: 7, 488–92.

Patel, V., Flisher, A.J., Hetrick, S. and McGorry, P. (2007) Mental Health of Young People: A Global Public-Health Challenge. *Lancet*, 369: 9569, 1302–13.

Richardson, N., Clarke, N. and Fowler, C. (2013) *A Report on the All-Ireland Young Men and Suicide Project.* Ireland: Men's Health Forum in Ireland.

Schubotz, D. (2009) *Getting away from the hurt?* ARK Research Update 60, Belfast: ARK. Accessed Sept. 2013 at: www.ark.ac.uk/publications/updates/update60.pdf

Schubotz, D. (2010) *The Mental and Emotional Health of 16-Year Olds in Northern Ireland. Evidence from the Young Life and Times Survey.* Belfast: Patient and Client Council. Accessed Sept. 2013 at: www.patientclientcouncil.hscni.net/uploads/research/The_mental_and_emotional_health_of_16_year_olds_in_NI.pdf

Tomlinson, M. (2007) *The Trouble with Suicide: Mental Health, Suicide and the Northern Ireland Conflict – A Review of the Evidence.* Belfast: School of Sociology, Social Policy and Social Work, Queen's University Belfast.

Tomlinson, M. (2012) War, Peace and Suicide: The Case of Northern Ireland. *International Sociology*, 27: 4, 464–82.

UNICEF (2007) *Child Poverty in Perspective: An Overview of Child Well-Being in Rich Countries. Innocenti Report Card 7.* Florence: UNICEF Innocenti Research Centre.

UNICEF (2013) *Child Well-being in Rich Countries: A Comparative Overview. Innocenti Report Card 11*. Florence: UNICEF Office of Research.

Wilkinson, R.G. and Pickett, K. (2009) *The Spirit Level: Why More Equal Societies Almost Always Do Better*. London: Allen Lane.

CHAPTER 4

Adolescent Loneliness in Northern Ireland

Mark Shevlin and Siobhan Murphy

Introduction

The aim of this chapter is to provide an overview of adolescent loneliness in Northern Ireland. Research has consistently demonstrated that loneliness, in particular adolescent loneliness, is an important problem with serious negative outcomes. Loneliness in the context of Northern Ireland may be of particular interest due to the history of political conflict and civil unrest which has led to social segregation between the two prominent communities (Catholic and Protestant). Previous research has confirmed that the community division in Northern Ireland has not just been a political issue but an inter-generational and socially structuring experience (Morrow, 2008). This chapter will examine loneliness in terms of prevalence, causes and psychological correlates, and discuss the findings of the 2011 Young Life and Times (YLT) survey. These findings will then be contextualised in light of empirical research conducted on loneliness both at a national and international level.

What is loneliness?

Loneliness is a universal experience: the consequence of a fundamental need for social connection (Cacioppo and Patrick, 2008). People can experience loneliness at any point in their lives and these experiences are usually transient and often the result of individual situations. However, for some, loneliness can be a chronic experience that can have negative consequences across a variety of domains. Loneliness has been defined as:

> ... *the unpleasant experience that occurs when a person's network of social relations is deficient in some important way, either quantitatively or qualitatively.*
>
> (Perlman and Peplau, 1981: 31)

Theoretical models of loneliness highlight that loneliness is a preceding factor of low mood and negative self-beliefs that are characteristics often seen in depression (Rubin, Coplan and Bowker, 2009) and research evidence shows that social withdrawal is evident in childhood (Rubin et al., 1995) and precedes the average age of the development of anxiety (14 years) and mood disorders (32 years) in Northern Ireland (Bunting et al., 2011).

Qualitative characteristics of loneliness reflect subjective appraisals of inter-personal relationships, such as level of satisfaction with relationships or perceived social acceptance. Quantitative characteristics, on the other hand, reflect more objective appraisals, such as frequency of contact or the number of friends an individual has (Heinrich and Gullone, 2006). Research has indicated that the subjective nature of relationship quality is a better predictor of loneliness rather than quantitative experiences (Cutrona, 1982). However, looking at both the qualitative and quantitative aspects of loneliness can improve understanding of the overall construct of loneliness. These differences also highlight that loneliness is distinct from an objective state of solitude, social isolation and being alone, and research has consistently focused on these underlying differences (De Jong Gierveld, Van Tilburg and Dykstra 2006; Larson, 1999).

It is also important to note that some individuals may be happy to spend time alone and not experience loneliness, whereas others may have large social networks and yet be unhappy within their relationships with others. This is particularly relevant to adolescents as research has demonstrated that during this developmental time young people do spend more time alone and use this time for identity reflection (Larson, 1999). Research further suggests that lonely and non-lonely individuals do not differ in terms of their daily structure or time spent alone (Hawkley et al., 2003). This indicates that social contact does not protect against loneliness; rather, it is the subjective experience of an individual's perception of the quality of their social interactions with others that is likely to lead to feelings of loneliness. Loneliness, therefore becomes a cause for concern when it induces a persistent pattern of negative thoughts, sensations and behaviours (Cacioppo and Patrick, 2008).

Theoretical perspectives on loneliness

There are numerous perspectives on loneliness that each provide useful interpretations of how and why feelings of loneliness can occur. The cognitive discrepancy model of loneliness was developed to shed light on the distinction between loneliness and social isolation. This model posits that people develop internal expectations against which they judge their interpersonal relationships with others. If someone perceives their relationships with others to fulfil this expectation then they are satisfied with their relationships and do not experience feelings of loneliness. However, if they are dissatisfied with their relationships and feel they do not meet this expectation then there is an increased likelihood of loneliness (Russell et al. 2012). An interactionist approach emphasises the role that personal, situational and cultural factors can play in the development of feelings of loneliness. This approach highlights that personality traits such as shyness or introversion and social anxiety interact with cultural and situational features that can deter the development and maintenance of social relationships (Heinrich and Gullone, 2006). Sociocognitive theories have recently demonstrated that lonely individuals can misconstrue social signals and perceive interactions with others to be more threatening and negative. Lonely individuals are also argued to possess unfavourable social impressions of others (Cacioppo and Patrick, 2008; Hawkley and Cacioppo, 2010) which in turn may lead to avoidance of social encounters and an increased risk of loneliness.

Prevalence of loneliness in childhood and adolescence

Loneliness is a common experience across the lifespan, with 80 per cent of children and adolescents and 40 per cent of people over 65 years reporting occasional loneliness. For 15 to 30 percent of people this can be persistent (Hawkley and Cacioppo, 2010) and emotionally painful (Brennan, 1982). Research has further demonstrated that loneliness is most prevalent during adolescence (Hawkley and Cacioppo, 2010). This is evidenced from a recent study by the *National Society for the Prevention of Cruelty to Children* (NSPCC): during April 2008 to March 2009 approximately 10,000 children contacted *Childline* regarding loneliness-related problems (Hutchinson and Woods, 2010). Adolescent loneliness therefore is an important issue, but has not been the focus of research in Northern Ireland. The Health Behaviour in School-Aged Children Study (1997–1998) included a single question on loneliness, and six per cent of males and 17 per cent of females (aged 15 years) reported being lonely in Northern Ireland (Scheidt et al., 2000). However, estimating prevalence on a single question does not adequately reflect a comprehensive assessment of adolescent loneliness.

Possible causes of loneliness

Adolescence is a time of transition from reliance on family members to a more independent life, with the establishment of a broader range of friends and intimate relationships. Loneliness has been shown to have a negative effect on the development of the social skills that are required for this transition to autonomy and individuality. Children who are lonely tend to have more difficulty initiating contact with peers, have less social interaction, and are viewed as less socially competent (Coplan, Closson, and Arbeau, 2007). Subsequently, they are more likely to experience rejection from their peer group and remain isolated into adolescence (Schwartz, Snidman, and Kagan, 1999). Therefore, adolescence is an ideal time to focus research and intervention efforts prior to the onset of these negative self-beliefs, behaviours, and attitudes becoming embedded and extending feelings of loneliness into adulthood (Heinrich and Gullone, 2006).

Peer victimisation (bullying) and family influences have been consistently associated with higher levels of loneliness in adolescents resulting in negative psychological adjustment, self-perceptions and perceived social status. Research has established that perceptions of early relationships that lack care/warmth, or overprotective environments, can be associated with a wide variety of interpersonal, psychological difficulties and feelings of loneliness (Gilbert and Perris, 2000). Jackson (2007) conducted a study on a sample of 281 adolescents to investigate the impact of self-presentation (characterised by fear of negative evaluation and social competence), parenting, peer relations and social anxiety on feelings of loneliness. The results found that young people who perceived negative evaluations from others and reported low social competence had higher levels of loneliness. Results further found that experiencing the family environment as being overprotective and lacking warmth increased feelings of loneliness. This study provides evidence of how negative beliefs of the self, such as viewing the self as incompetent and fear of negative evaluations of others can also contribute to feelings of loneliness. Segrin et al. (2012) investigated parental loneliness, familial environment and bullying as potential predictors of young adults' loneliness. Results confirmed that both parental loneliness and a history of being bullied were significant predictors of loneliness. The study found that being from an open and expressive family environment was associated with lower feelings of loneliness. Parental loneliness was found to both directly and indirectly affect young adult loneliness. Segrin et al. argue that these findings are indicative that lonely parents have dual influence on their children's loneliness, both directly (by genetic transmission) and indirectly (through an unsupportive family environment). Exposure to bullying in adolescence was also found to significantly predict loneliness in young adults.

Psychological factors associated with loneliness

Loneliness has been linked to a range of social, psychological, and academic problems. Research indicates that loneliness has been shown to be a significant predictor of poor quality peer interactions and peer relationships (Chen et al., 2006), negative self-concept and low self-esteem (Brage, Meredith and Woodward, 1993), disorders such as anxiety, depression, and phobias (Heinrich and Gullone, 2006), personality disorders and psychosis (ibid) and dislike of school and poor academic achievement (Larson, 1999). A relationship between loneliness and physical health has also been identified: with loneliness being associated with poorer physical health and higher need of health care services (Hawkley and Cacioppo, 2010).

The association between loneliness and mental health problems originates, and is strongest, during adolescence. Lasgaard and colleagues (2011) investigated associations between loneliness in different relationship domains and indicators of mental health problems. In this Danish national study of 1009 high school students three types of loneliness (peer-related, family-related and romantic-related) and six indicators of psychological difficulties (depression, anxiety, self-harm, suicide ideation, eating disorders and social phobia) were examined. Results found that peer and family-related loneliness was significantly associated with depression, anxiety and suicide ideation. Family-related loneliness was also associated with self-harm and eating disorders. Social phobia, on the other hand was predicted by both peer-related and romantic-related loneliness.

There have been numerous large scale studies of adolescents in Europe that have demonstrated the links between loneliness and depressive symptoms. For example, Vanhalst et al. (2012a) examined the course of loneliness from mid to late adolescence across five time points in a sample of 389 adolescents aged 15 to 20 years. The aim of that study was to examine differences in loneliness over time on the basis of demographic and personality traits at age 15 and psychosocial functioning at age 20. Results revealed that loneliness decreased over time. This study also identified five subgroups of adolescents (low loneliness, low increasing, moderate decreasing, high increasing and persistently high loneliness). The majority of adolescents fell into the low loneliness subgroup, which meant they did not report feelings of loneliness, and displayed higher levels of peer functioning and academic adjustment. These adolescents were also found to be more extraverted, agreeable and emotionally stable with higher self-esteem and low levels of depression, anxiety and stress. Conversely, individuals in the persistently high loneliness subgroup were characterised by low levels of agreeableness and emotional stability. These adolescents also reported poor self-esteem, higher levels of depression, stress and anxiety and social phobia. Empirical research has therefore provided useful insights into the psychological consequences of loneliness. However, these studies have failed to determine if loneliness is associated with clinically-meaningful levels of psychological problems, or whether the association exists only in the non-clinical range.

Adolescent loneliness in Northern Ireland: The Young Life and Times survey

The main part of this chapter is based on data from the 2011 YLT survey. Participants were asked a range of demographic questions, such as gender, ethnicity, area of residence, school type attended, community religion, and physical disability. Participants were also asked: *'How well-off do you think your family is financially?'* based on response categories (1) Not-at-all well-off, (2) Not-very-well-off, (3) Average, (4) Well-off, (5) Very well off. (For more details about the questions asked and how to access information on survey, see the Technical Appendix at the end of this book.)

The UCLA Loneliness Scale (UCLA-LS: Russell, 1996) is the most widely used self-report assessment tools for both adolescent and adult loneliness. It consists of 20 items (11 positive and 9 negative) that are rated on a four-point Likert scale. The response format corresponds to the frequency of feelings of loneliness, ranging from *never* (1) to *often* (4). The total score is the sum of all 20 items, and ranges from 20 to 80, with higher scores reflecting greater feelings of loneliness. All negatively worded items were reversed. In an attempt to avoid socially desirable responses the items do not refer directly to loneliness. Instead the items capture a range of opinions regarding an individual's social networks, for example, *'There are people I can talk to'* and *'There are people I can turn to'*. Scores greater than 42 indicate loneliness.

The General Health Questionnaire-12 (GHQ-12: Goldberg and Williams, 1998) is a 12-item self-report psychiatric screening measure designed to identify individuals at risk of developing mental health problems (see also Davidson's chapter in this book). The measure is scored using a four-point Likert scale: *better than usual* (0), *same as usual* (1), *less than usual* (2), *much less than usual* (3). The potential range of scores using this method ranges from 0 to 36, with higher scores being indicative of greater psychological distress. The GHQ-12 has been argued to measure three constructs that tap into feelings of anxiety and depression for example '*feeling constantly under strain*'. It also measures social problems, for example: '*Have you recently been able to enjoy your day to day activities?*' Finally it measures loss of confidence, for example '*thinking of yourself as a worthless person*'. In this chapter, the full GHQ-12 will used as a general measure of potential mental health problems.

Who is lonely?

Table 4.1 indicates that 16 year olds in Northern Ireland typically report low levels of loneliness. There were small differences between males' and females' loneliness scores with females scoring slightly higher. It was found that home status, that is, whether respondents lived with both parents or not, did not predict loneliness. Although adolescents from single parent backgrounds did report higher levels of loneliness, the difference was small and was not significant. However, variables that did significantly impact on loneliness were being from an ethnic minority, and having a disability. These findings are consistent with other studies that have examined these issues in regards to loneliness.

Table 4.2 shows that there were only small differences in UCLA loneliness scores depending on where the participants lived. This suggests that urbanicity has a limited role in predicting adolescent loneliness in Northern Ireland. However, there were larger differences in terms of socio-economic status.

Table 4.1   Mean scores on the UCLA loneliness measure for a range of predictor variables

UCLA Score	Number	Mean
Gender		
Male	641	32.64
Female	774	33.01
Ethnic minority		
Yes	154	34.79
No	1170	32.74
Home status		
Both parents	1033	32.57
Single parent	352	33.57
Disability		
Yes	155	35.57
No	1252	32.53

Source: 2011 YLT survey

Table 4.2 UCLA Loneliness Scores by urbanicity and socio-economic status

UCLA Score	Number	Mean
Area of residence		
Big city	107	33.52
Suburbs	196	33.87
Small city/town	564	32.15
Village	226	32.72
Farm/country	298	33.04
Total	1391	32.78
Socio-economic status		
Not-at-all-well-off	58	32.76
Not-very-well-off	210	35.71
Average-well-off	789	32.61
Well-off	291	31.77
Very-well-off	14	31.21
Don't know	45	30.80
Total	1407	32.83

Source: 2011 YLT survey

Table 4.2 shows that perceiving family economic status as being '*not-very-well-off*' significantly increased scores on the UCLA loneliness measure.

There were differences on loneliness scores depending on religious affiliation. Table 4.3 indicates slight differences between Catholic and Protestant scores, with Protestants having elevated scores on the UCLA Loneliness Scale.

Table 4.3 UCLA Loneliness Scores and religious affiliation

UCLA Score	Number	Mean
Religious area		
Mainly Catholic	421	32.07
Mainly Protestant	457	33.29
Mixed area	489	32.59
Total	1367	32.82
Religion		
Catholic	586	31.88
Protestant	511	32.26
No religion	314	35.39
Total	1407	32.81

Source: 2011 YLT survey

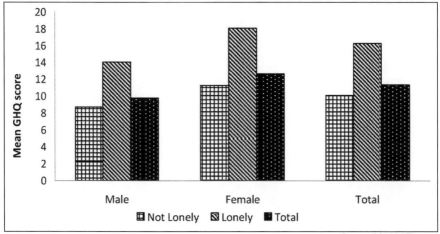

Source: 2011 YLT survey

Figure 4.1   GHQ-12 scores, by loneliness and gender

However, for those participants who did not affiliate themselves to any religion there was a marked increase in the UCLA scale. This suggests that feeling connected to a religious denomination may act as a protective factor against feelings of loneliness.

Figure 4.1 depicts the pattern of mean GHQ scores for males and females, and for lonely and non-lonely adolescents. Overall, lonely male and female adolescents scored higher on the GHQ than their non-lonely counterparts. This suggests that loneliness is associated with poorer mental health, and the association appears to be stronger for females.

Discussion of YLT findings

The mean UCLA Loneliness score among the 1,434 YLT respondents was 32.82. In comparison to other countries this rate of loneliness was lower than reported in a review of adolescent samples using the same measure (Lasgaard, 2006). It was found that ethnicity, disability, poverty and lack of religious affiliation were all predictors of loneliness. As previously stated, research has indicated the importance of examining situational and cultural factors in regards to loneliness. To some extent, these findings can be interpreted using an interactionist perspective to loneliness that acknowledges the cultural and situational factors in the development of loneliness.

There is increasing interest in ethnic communities' mental and social well being in recent years, due to a significant increase in rates of immigration to

Northern Ireland since 2004. During the period from July 2000 to June 2009 there were an estimated 110,000 long-term international migrants settled in Northern Ireland (Russell, 2011). Scharf, Phillipson and Smith (2004) previously revealed that high levels of social exclusion and neighbourhood exclusion in socially-deprived areas in the United Kingdom (UK) indicated that those at greatest risk for exclusion and loneliness were individuals from ethnic minorities. Supporting these earlier findings, the 2011 YLT data show that being from a minority ethnic group significantly increased loneliness scores.

Northern Ireland is a country that remains, to some degree, segregated with opposing religious, cultural and political differences (see Devine's chapter in this volume for a detailed discussion of this). Therefore, an outsider coming into this climate may experience the more intense feelings of social disconnection that stem from not affiliating to either community. Also, the 2011 YLT survey showed that having a disability had a significant impact on feelings of loneliness, and this is similar to what has been found in other countries (Lasgaard, Goossens and Elklit, 2010). Finally, another significant finding of the study was that adolescents who perceived their family as less well-off had higher levels of loneliness. A possible explanation for these findings may be that adolescents from less well-off backgrounds may not have the same opportunity to engage in frequent social activities outside the school environment as adolescents from more financially-secure backgrounds. This could have the effect of increasing feelings of social disconnection from their peer group and feeling like they are missing out or being left out.

Loneliness and mental health

Previous YLT surveys have investigated the mental and emotional health of adolescents (for example, see Lloyd et al., 2008). In the 2004, 2005 and 2006 surveys it was demonstrated that between 20 and 24 per cent of respondents reported psychological distress as measured by the GHQ-12. Shevlin et al. (2013) further analysed the 2011 YLT data to examine the association between loneliness and psychiatric morbidity in Northern Irish adolescents using the GHQ-12. That study used the GHQ method of scoring, which counts the number of 'problem' items selected by the respondent completing the GHQ-12. The mean score was 2.44, and 28.4 per cent of respondents scored greater than three. As previously cited, the mean UCLA Loneliness score was 32.82 and 15.6 per cent scored greater than 42 indicating elevated feelings of loneliness. Previous YLT surveys that have focused on mental health problems had failed to examine the potential confounding influences of demographic

variables such as socio-economic status, family structure and religion. Therefore, this study included a number of these variables to examine the effects
they may have on mental well-being. The results show that significant
predictors of psychological distress were being female, living in poverty, and
loneliness. The results further indicate that high levels of loneliness was the
greatest predictor of psychological distress and that lonely young people were
over five times more likely to have poorer mental health outcomes than those
who were not lonely. This finding supports previous work on the psychological
consequences of loneliness on mental well-being. For example, high feelings of
loneliness have been found to be associated with depression and anxiety
(Lasgaard, Goossens and Elklit, 2011), and with emotional instability (Vanhalst
et al., 2012). Loneliness has further been associated with more severe mental
health outcomes such as personality disorders and psychosis (Heinrich and
Gullone, 2006).

Do community relations play a protective role against loneliness?

An interesting finding from this survey is that adolescent loneliness in Northern
Ireland is significantly lower than in other countries. A possible reason for this
is the political violence that Northern Ireland has experienced. As discussed in
Devine's chapter in this volume, Northern Ireland to this day still remains a
largely segregated society with two separate communities holding different
national identities, and with segregated housing and schools. This intra-group
cohesiveness may in turn have the impact of reducing adolescent loneliness for
the majority of young people in comparison to young people in other countries.
Rokach and colleagues have repeatedly demonstrated the cultural differences
that can affect how individuals express and cope with loneliness (for example,
Rokach and Neto, 2005; Rokach et al., 2001). In one such study they examined
loneliness in Croatian and Canadian populations, and found that Croatians
reported lower levels of loneliness than their Canadian counterparts (Rokach et
al., 2001). This finding may be attributable to the fact that Croatia, like
Northern Ireland, is a country that has been closely connected with political
conflict and strong national identities which may act as a protective factor in
feelings of loneliness. Furthermore, recent research conducted in the UK
suggests that community relations and community ties may have a protective
role against negative outcomes such as loneliness, social exclusion and
isolation. These findings support a recent survey commissioned by the BBC that
interviewed 1,000 adults regarding loneliness and found that 27 per cent of

adults living in London reported feeling lonely *often* or *all of the time* (BBC, 2012). This survey also found that 28 per cent reported little or no sense of community in their area which further supports how poor community ties can contribute to feelings of loneliness.

Overall, the findings of the 2011 YLT survey are positive in that they show that there are generally low levels of adolescent loneliness in Northern Ireland. However, those who are lonely have an increased risk of mental health problems.

Interventions

A recent review showed that interventions, aimed at changing maladaptive social cognitions, were effective in reducing loneliness (Masi et al., 2010). Given the stability of loneliness from childhood to adolescence (Rubin, Coplan and Bowker, 2009), primary school-based interventions, with or without parental involvement, may be most appropriate. Interventions based on social skills training, peer-pairing, and cognitive behavioural principles have all been shown to be effective in promoting positive social interactions (Greco and Morris, 2001).

Research conducted in Europe has confirmed that interventions that are directed towards helping lonely individuals develop satisfying social relationships have been effective. These types of interventions can help individuals improve on their social skills and work on dysfunctional appraisals that may be present, such as fear of rejection. For example, the *Friendship Enrichment Program* (FEP) was developed in the Netherlands with the aim of teaching individuals to nourish friendships and promote making new friendships. This programme has been found to be successful in alleviating feelings of loneliness in older individuals (De Jong Gierveld, van Tilburg and Dykstra, 2006). This could be integrated through school interventions to target childhood and adolescent loneliness. Teaching children and adolescents skills that may improve how they interact with others and how they perceive their relationships may be a successful mechanism in alleviating feelings of loneliness. Within the UK, the Department of Health has funded *The Campaign to End Loneliness* after recognition of the negative outcomes associated with feelings of loneliness on social, mental and physical well-being. Whilst again this campaign is targeted towards older adults, it works through developing research, policy, campaigning and innovation to combat loneliness. This campaign promotes the importance of social connection in later life and could be targeted towards loneliness-related problems in adolescence.

Future directions

Past research into adolescent loneliness has predominantly centred on the 'Triple P' of peers, parents and personality in the development and maintenance of loneliness (Goossens, 2012). However, loneliness is now being recognised as a complex phenotype, with multiple environmental and biological factors influencing its onset and developmental course (Van Roekel et al., 2010). Recent research has been looking at more integrative approaches to the understanding and developmental course of loneliness by incorporating multiple research disciplines. These include looking at how genetic and environmental influences can contribute to the understanding of loneliness. Research methods utilised in neurosciences have also recently been applied to the investigation of lonely individuals through the use of eye-tracking techniques and diary studies that involve monitoring day to day interactions (Goossens, 2012). These new multilevel analytical methods are expected to shed new light into the true nature of loneliness through gene × environment interactions and may act as a catalyst to future research endeavours.

References

BBC (2012) *Lonely London: Poll Suggests a Quarter Feel Alone*. BBC news Online, 20 November. Accessed 18.7.2013 at www.bbc.co.uk/news/uk-england-london-20324373

Brage, D., Meredith, W. and Woodward, J. (1993) Correlates of Loneliness Among Midwestern Adolescents. *Adolescence*, 28: 111, 685–93.

Brennan, T. (1982) Loneliness at Adolescence. In Peplau, L.A. and Perlman, D. (Eds.) *Loneliness: A Sourcebook of Current Theory, Research and Therapy.* New York: Wiley.

Bunting, B.P. et al. (2011) Lifetime Prevalence of Mental Health Disorders and Delay in Treatment Following Initial Onset: Evidence From the Northern Ireland Study of Health and Stress. *Psychological Medicine*, 42: 8, 1727–39.

Cacioppo, J. and Patrick, W. (2008) *Loneliness. Human Nature and the Need for Social Connection.* New York: Norton.

Chen, X. et al. (2006) Reticent Behaviour and Experiences in Peer Interactions in Canadian and Chinese Children. *Developmental Psychology*, 42, 656–65.

Coplan, R., Closson, L. and Arbeau, K. (2007) Gender Differences in The Behavioural Associates of Loneliness and Social Dissatisfaction in Kindergarten. *Journal of Child Psychology and Psychiatry*, 48: 10, 988–95.

Cutrona, C.E. (1982) Transition to College: Loneliness and The Process of Social Adjustment. In: Peplau, L.A. and Perlman, D. (Eds.) *Loneliness: A Sourcebook of Current Theory, Research and Therapy.* New York: Wiley.

De Jong Gierveld, J., van Tilburg, T. and Dykstra, P. (2006) Loneliness and Social Isolation. In: Vangelisti A. and Perlman, D. (Eds.) *Cambridge Handbook of Personal Relationships.* Cambridge: Cambridge University Press.

Gilbert, P. and Perris, C. (2000) Early Experiences and Subsequent Psychosocial Adaptation. An Introduction. *Clinical Psychology and Psychotherapy*, 7: 4, 243–5.

Goldberg, D.P. and Williams, P. (1998) *A User's Guide to the General Health Questionnaire*. Windsor: NFER-Nelson.

Goossens, L. (2012) Genes, Environments, and Interactions as a New Challenge For European Developmental Psychology: The Sample Case of Adolescent Loneliness. *European Journal of Developmental Psychology*, 9: 4, 432–45.

Greco, L. and Morris, T. (2001) Treating Childhood Shyness and Related Behavior: Empirically Evaluated Approaches to Promote Positive Social Interactions. *Clinical Child and Family Psychology Review*, 4: 4, 299–318.

Hawkley, L.C. et al. (2003) Loneliness in Everyday Life: Cardiovascular Activity, Psychosocial Context, and Health Behaviours. *Journal of Personality and Social Psychology*, 85: 1, 105–20.

Hawkley, L.C. and Cacioppo, J.T. (2010) Loneliness Matters: A Theoretical and Empirical Review of Consequences and Mechanisms. *Annals of Behavioural Medicine*, 40: 2, 218–27.

Heinrich, L. and Gullone, E. (2006) The Clinical Significance of Loneliness: A Literature Review. *Clinical Psychology Review*, 26: 6, 695–718.

Hutchinson, D. and Woods, R. (2010) *Children Talking to Childline About Loneliness*. London: NSPCC. Accessed Sept. 2013 at: www.nspcc.org.uk/inform/publications/casenotes/clcasenotes_loneliness_wdf74260.pdf

Jackson, T. (2007) Protective Self-Presentation, Sources of Socialisation and Loneliness Among Australian Adolescents and Young Adults. *Personality and Individual Differences*, 43: 6, 1552–62.

Larson, R.W. (1999) The Uses of Loneliness in Adolescence. In: Rotenberg, K.J. and Hymel, S. (Eds.) *Loneliness in Childhood and Adolescence*. Cambridge: Cambridge University Press.

Lasgaard, M. (2006) Lonely Among Others: A Psychological Investigation of Loneliness in Young People in Denmark. *Psykologisk Studieskriftserie*, 9, 1–131.

Lasgaard, M., Goossens, L. and Elklit, A. (2011) Loneliness, Depressive Symptomatology and Suicide Ideation in Adolescence: Cross-Sectional and Longitudinal Analysis. *Journal of Abnormal Child Psychology*, 39: 1, 137–50.

Lasgaard, M. et al. (2010) Loneliness and Social Support in Adolescent Boys with Autism Spectrum Disorders. *Journal of Autism and Developmental Disorders*, 40: 2, 218–26.

Lloyd, K. et al. (2008) Adolescent Mental Health in Northern Ireland: Empirical Evidence From The Young Life and Times Survey. In: Schubotz, D. and Devine, P. (Eds.) *Young People in Post-Conflict Northern Ireland. The Past Cannot Be Changed But The Future Can Be Developed*. Lyme Regis: Russell House Publishing.

Masi, C.M. et al. (2010) A Meta-Analysis of Interventions to Reduce Loneliness. *Personality and Social Psychology*, 15: 3, 219–66.

Morrow, D. (2008) Shared or Scared? Attitudes to Community Relations Among Young People 2003–2007. In: Schubotz, D. and Devine, P. (Eds.) *Young People in Post-Conflict Northern Ireland. The Past Cannot Be Changed But The Future Can Be Developed*. Lyme Regis: Russell House Publishing.

Perlman, D. and Peplau, L. (1981) Toward a Social Psychology of Loneliness. In: Duck, S.W. and Gilmour, R. (Eds.) *Personal Relationships 3: Personal Relationships in Disorder*. London: Academic Press.

Rokach, A. and Neto, F. (2005) Age, Culture, and The Antecedents of Loneliness. *Social Behavior and Personality*, 33: 5, 477–94.

Rokach, A. et al. (2001) The Effects of Culture on The Meaning of Loneliness. *Social Indicators Research*, 53: 1, 17–31.

Rubin, K., Coplan, R. and Bowker, J. (2009) Social Withdrawal in Childhood. *Annual Review of Psychology*, 60, 141–71.

Rubin, K.H. et al. (1995) The Waterloo Longitudinal Project: Predicting Adolescent Internalizing and Externalizing Problems From Early and Mid-Childhood. *Developmental Psychopathology*, 7: 4, 751–64.

Russell, D. (1996) UCLA Loneliness Scale (Version 3): Reliability, Validity, and Factor Structure. *Journal of Personality Assessment*, 66: 1, 20–40.

Russell, D., Cutrona, C., McRae, C. and Gomez, M. (2012) Is Loneliness the Same as Being Alone? *The Journal of Psychology: Interdisciplinary and Applied*, 146: 1–2, 7–22.

Russell, R. (2011) *Migration in Northern Ireland: A Demographic Perspective*. Research Paper 71/11. Belfast: Northern Ireland Assembly Research and Information Service.

Scharf, T., Phillipson, C. and Smith, A.E. (2004) Poverty and Social Exclusion: Growing Older in Deprived Urban Neighbourhoods. In: Walker, A. and Hagan Hennessy, C. (Eds.) *Growing Older: Quality of Life in Old Age*. Maidenhead: Open University Press.

Scheidt, P. et al. (2000) Adolescents General Health and Wellbeing. In: Currie, C. et al. (Eds.) *Health and Health Behaviour Among Young People.* Health Policy for Children and Adolescents' Number 1, Copenhagen: World Health Organization.

Schwartz, C.E., Snidman, N. and Kagan, J. (1999) Adolescent Social Anxiety as an Outcome of Inhibited Temperament in Childhood. *Journal of the American Academy of Child & Adolescent Psychiatry*, 38: 8, 1008–15.

Segrin, C. et al. (2012) Family of Origin Environment and Adolescent Bullying Predict Young Adult Loneliness. *The Journal of Applied Psychology: Interdisciplinary and Applied*, 146: 1–2, 119–34.

Shevlin, M. et al. (2013) Adolescent Loneliness and Psychiatric Morbidity in Northern Ireland. *British Journal of Clinical Psychology*, 52: 2, 230–4.

Vanhalst, J. et al. (2012a) The Development of Loneliness From Mid to Late Adolescence: Trajectory Classes, Personality Traits and Psychosocial Functioning. *Journal of Adolescence* [e-publication ahead of print].

Vanhalst, J. et al. (2012b) The Interplay of Loneliness and Depressive Symptoms Across Adolescence: Exploring The Role of Personality Traits. *Journal of Youth and Adolescence*, 41: 6, 776–87.

Van Roekel, E. et al. (2010) Loneliness in Adolescence: Gene × Environment Interactions Involving The Serotonin Transporter Gene. *Journal of Child Psychology and Psychiatry*, 51: 7, 747–54.

CHAPTER 5

Play Matters

Jacqueline O'Loughlin

The main characteristic of play – child or adult – is not its content, but its mode. Play is an approach to action, not a form of activity.

Jerome Bruner, quoted in Moyles (1989)

Introduction

Children and young people have a wealth of situated knowledge about their experiences and environments, and about how space, time and attitudes shape and impact on everyday interactions. When children are asked about what they think is important in their lives, playing and hanging out with friends is usually at the top of the list. Widely recognised as integral to the acquisition and development of skills and competencies, play contributes greatly to children's holistic development. In play, children learn societal roles, norms and values and develop physical and cognitive competencies such as creativity, self-worth and efficacy. The issues impacting upon children's right to play and their ability to play out freely in their neighbourhoods are not limited to socio-economic conditions, or levels of technological development, but are quickly becoming worldwide concerns, increasingly preoccupying people wherever they live.

In 2010, to coincide with the development of Northern Ireland's *Play and Leisure Implementation Plan*, the Office of the First Minister and Deputy Minister (OFMDFM) part-funded the Young Life and Times (YLT) survey in order to facilitate direct engagement with young people on questions pertaining to their play and leisure experiences. Working with OFMDFM officials and ARK, *PlayBoard* – Northern Ireland's leading NGO for Play – assisted in the formulation of questions for inclusion in the survey. Analysis of the 2010 YLT findings referenced throughout this chapter resulted in an ARK Research Update entitled *Playscapes at 16* (O'Loughlin, Stevenson and Schubotz, 2011) and in a further briefing paper containing a more comprehensive analysis (Schubotz and McCooey, 2013).

This chapter comprises data and narrative based on the 2010 YLT survey to highlight the most pertinent play and leisure issues impacting upon the lives of young people living in Northern Ireland. The lens of the YLT survey is used to contextualise the role and function of play in debates on social policy, rights and childhood. The terms *play* and *leisure* are used interchangeably and may be considered as any autonomous unstructured activity or combination of activities that a child or young person freely engages in. The use of the term *child* refers to the age definition as espoused by the United Nations Convention on the Rights of the Child (UNCRC, 1989) that is, up to the age of 18 years, or up to 21 years where they have a disability.

Play is an inherent and deeply rooted element of the life cycle of human beings. As a generic and ubiquitous term, it can be applied to a wide range of behaviours and activities that both children and adults engage in when they have free discretionary time. According to Rennie (2003: 22) play can be physical, intellectual, solitary, risky, social or even scary, but '*in retrospect it is always remembered as fun*'. As many commentators have noted, the holistic and multi-dimensional benefits of play and playing have salience throughout the lifespan (Lester and Russell, 2008).

Play takes many forms and deals with a raft of emotions: curiosity, creativity, pleasure and contemplation, or even fear. Commonly aligned with childhood culture, it is easy to recognise, but notoriously difficult to define (Ellis, 1973; Levy, 1978; Sutton-Smith, 2001; Lester and Russell, 2010). According to Lester and Russell (2010: xi) 'adults have different and often contradictory explanations of the nature and value of play'. Some adults may ignore it, or dismiss it as a waste of time; some may curb it, especially in the teenage years, where it may be viewed as anti-social, dangerous or subversive; while others chose to appropriate it as a learning or socialisation mechanism. Definition aside, the evidence is clear that play is a dominant and integral aspect of all human learning and interaction. Regardless of age, culture or socio-economic status, play, playing and playfulness are closely aligned with our innate need for self-expression, exploration and learning.

Right to play

Play is an entitlement of childhood. Children's play is first and foremost a matter of human rights, as enshrined in the UNCRC. The Convention provides an internationally accepted standard that is to be applied to the basic human rights affecting all children. In ratifying the UNCRC in 1991, the United Kingdom (UK) Government, acting as a State Party, agreed to protect and enhance the basic rights of children through its polices, programmes and services.

The right to play and leisure as articulated in Article 31 of the UNCRC asserts that every child and young person under the age of 18 years has the right to engage in age-appropriate play and leisure activities. Article 31 reads:

1. *State Parties recognise the right of the child to rest and leisure, to engage in play and recreational activities appropriate to the age of the child and to participate freely in cultural life and the arts.*
2. *State Parties shall respect and promote the right of the child to participate fully in cultural and artistic life and shall encourage provision of appropriate and equal opportunities for cultural, artistic recreational and leisure activities.*

As a discrete element of Article 31, play shares a footing with other rights, such as rest, leisure, recreational activities, cultural life and the arts. Viewed collectively, these rights describe the necessary conditions required to both support and protect the unique and evolving nature of childhood. The findings from the 2010 YLT survey support this view, with 95 per cent of young people aged 16 reporting that play, hanging out with friends, having free time and being able to choose what to do in their free time was a very important aspect of their lives. The evidence from YLT echoes the guidance offered in the latest General Comment by the United Nations Committee on the Rights of the Child (CRC, 2013: 5). This states that children 'need leisure, defined as time and space without obligations, entertainment or stimulus, which they can choose to fill as actively or inactively as the wish'. YLT respondents confirm that play activity in the teenage years entails hanging out with friends, listening to music, playing computer or simply being on their own, without being told what to do (O'Loughlin, Stevenson and Schubotz, 2011).

As noted in the General Comment 17 (GC-17), 'each element of Article 31 is mutually linked and reinforcing, and when realised, serves to enrich the lives of children' (CRC, 2013: 4). Whilst emphasising the intrinsic value of play to the child as being enjoyment, pleasure, learning and participation in everyday life; GC-17 further provides State Parties, both national and devolved administrations, with a timely reminder of the obligation they undertook when they ratified the UNCRC to guarantee that all rights, including those contained within Article 31, are respected, protected and fulfilled.

The health and well-being benefits of play extend through childhood and beyond, and GC-17 seeks to enhance this understanding. Our biology ordains play as the key mechanism for optimal learning and development (Lester and Russell, 2008). Play is:

> ... *essential to the health and well-being of children and young people; the development of creativity, imagination, self-confidence, self-efficacy and physical, social cognitive and emotional strength and skills.*
>
> (CRC, 2013: 5)

Play is perhaps a child's first free self-controlled activity, and in this context it is closely linked to how a child makes sense of the world. In play, children discover the difference between themselves and others, and these discoveries help children become independent, self-sufficient and autonomous, which according to business guru Daniel Pink is something that is highly prized. According to Pink (2009), autonomy has a profound effect on performance and attitude throughout all the spheres of human engagement, home, school, and community, including the work place.

Paradoxically, in contemporary society children have fewer opportunities for independent mobility and autonomous negotiation in their communities and neighbourhood. Natural opportunities for outdoor play are being eroded and are slowly diminishing (Beunderman, Hannon and Bradwell, 2007; Gill, 2007; Madge, 2006; Madge and Baker, 2007; Gladwin and Collins, 2008; Lester and Russell, 2008). In recent years, like most countries in the developed world, Northern Ireland has encountered its fair share of societal, economic and environmental constraints. These, along with technological advancements, have helped to impede children's ability to play outdoors. By way of example, commentators note factors such as the loss of green space and little or no access to nature in urban housing schemes. The designers and architects of our built environment and public spaces do not engage with children as end users; only two per cent of YLT respondents had directly been asked about facilities and spaces they use to play in by those who are responsible for the planning of these facilities, namely town planners, architects, developers or builders (see Figure 5.1). The survey showed that 91 per cent of YLT respondents felt that children and young people should, and indeed have the right to, be consulted

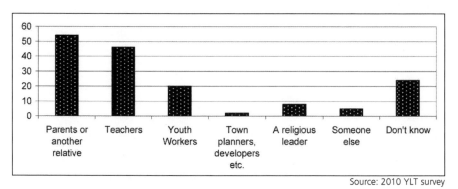

Source: 2010 YLT survey

Figure 5.1   Respondents saying their opinions about play and leisure facilities and spaces have been sought by the following adults (%)

about the design of spaces for play and leisure. A further 78 per cent disagreed that the design of these spaces should be left to adults only. This high proportion is particularly interesting as fewer than four in ten respondents (39%) said they had heard about the UNCRC, which establishes the right of children to be consulted in matters affecting them. In reality, a much smaller proportion of YLT respondents had ever been asked their opinion about leisure time activities, as Figure 5.1 shows. The findings also reveal that while parents and relatives were the group most likely to have asked young people about play spaces, still only just over half of respondents were asked their opinions by their parents and relatives.

It is no wonder that children say the built environment is unwelcoming and sometimes hostile. Negative messages and imagery in local communities support this perception: 'No ball games', 'Stay off the Grass', 'No loitering', 'No skateboarding here' – they might as well say 'no **children** welcome'. Allied to this discussion is society's consumerist penchant for the motorcar. The speed and volume of vehicles on the road aligned with the need to 'house' cars means that community spaces that once welcomed playing children are now, in the mainstay, the preferred place for the car. More and more children are growing up deprived of play space – deprived of play.

The impact of 'play deprivation' – a phrase coined by Bob Hughes – is concerning. Play deprivation, according to Hughes, is the result of either 'a chronic lack of sensory interaction with the world' or 'a neurotic, erratic interaction'. In other words:

> The child's play experience is so impoverished by lack of stimuli that they are forced to search within their own limited experience for the reality they need, or it is so subject to changes outside of the child's control that the child's view of the world is one of instability or neurosis.

(Hughes, 2003)

In essence, play deprivation leads to unhealthy, unfit, repressed and depressed children and young people.

It could be argued that Northern Ireland's turbulent past further compounds the concept of play deprivation. The prolonged political strife has caused and continues to cause trans-generational trauma. As discussed by Devine in the chapter on community relations within this book, the housing and schooling systems are strongly segregated. This has corralled and restricted children and young people's social mobility; where, how and with whom children and young people play is compromised (McAlister, Scraton and Haydon, 2010). Beckett (2010) picks this subject up in her study, suggesting that young people at play in Northern Ireland are segregated, demonised and marginalised. Consequently, their right to play is not adequately recognised and is even neglected; this disregard negatively impacts upon all other children's rights especially the child's right to protection.

Play in adolescence

Confirmed by the YLT findings, as children grow older, they need places that afford opportunities to socialise, to be with their peers or to be alone. As one 2010 YLT respondent put it, 'we need more youth clubs or places for teenagers to hang out, and not having them on the streets, giving themselves a bad name, when really they are just bored with nowhere to go'. The importance of leisure time activities for older children is emphasised by the World Health Organization (WHO), which states that participation in varied forms of recreational activities provides young people with outlets for self-expression and feelings of autonomy, which facilitate their ability to bond with adults and with one another, thus creating a sense of community and belonging (WHO, 2002).

Adolescence is an important transitional period; it is a time when young people undergo major adjustments, from changes in themselves to encountering changes in society, wherein altered expectations are experienced (Hendry et al., 1993). Change, or more specifically the speed of change, in the teenage years and the adaptations required can be problematic, and for some, can cause serious emotional and psychological problems. Older children and teenagers progressively explore more challenging opportunities for risk taking. As outlined in GC-17 of the UNCRC, these experiences are developmentally necessary for adolescents, contributing to their discovery of identity and belonging.

Framed through an adult lens, the behaviour of children, particularly teenagers, can at times be problematic for adults. Adolescent play will often appropriate, invert and subvert adult cultural expectations. Adults want play to act as a tool for socialisation or learning, whereas adolescents just want to play. At times, the play of older children will often transgress adult understanding and may be viewed by some as disruptive, threatening or even antisocial. The empirical results of the YLT survey unfortunately confirm the negative attitudes of many adults towards young people and the widely held disrespect and disregard for the way they spend their leisure time. The vast majority of YLT respondents (85%) said that they felt that young people are judged negatively just because they are young. Those who came from financially less well-off backgrounds were most likely to feel that young people were negatively judged because of their young age, with 88 per cent of these young people saying this. Furthermore, 79 per cent of respondents felt that the media portrays young people mostly negatively. This perception was universal among 16 year olds regardless of their background. Only three per cent of respondents felt that the media portrayed young people mostly positively.

However, respondents' personal experiences of whether or not they had been treated with disrespect and suspicion, were more varied by their social background and gender, as Table 5.1 shows. Whilst 82 per cent of YLT respondents said they had been treated with suspicion in shops, respondents from well-off backgrounds were much less likely to say this (76%). Males (37%) were more likely to have been excluded from shops than females (29%). Half of well-off respondents said that they had been told to move on by someone when standing with their friends on the street compared to nearly two thirds (66%) of respondents categorised as being from not so well-off families. Overall, residents were most likely to tell young people to move on (65%), followed by the police (40%) and community representatives (18%). Males were much more likely than females to have been told to move on by the police (50% and 35% respectively) whilst not well-off respondents (70%) were more likely than well-off respondents (62%) to say that residents had told them and their friends to move on.

Table 5.1   Respondents who said they experienced the following because they are a young person

	%					
	Gender		Financial family background			
	Males	Females	Not well-off	Average well-off	Well-off	All
Treated suspiciously by staff in shops	82	82	85	85	76	82
Told to leave schoolbag outside shops	75	71	74	69	76	72
Excluded from shops	37	29	34	29	34	32
Told to move on when standing on street with friends	58	56	66	56	50	56

Source: 2010 YLT survey

Many YLT respondents commented how angry and annoyed this made them feel, especially when they had 'not done anything wrong'. Some respondents commented that they 'had every right to be there', which made them feel unwanted, judged and even discriminated against.

Play and risk taking

Risk-taking and challenging play is used by older children to test, push and explore social, emotional and physical boundaries. In this way young people gain control over their attention processes, and acquire critical life skills, thus providing the social dexterity required for integration into their local communities (Larson and Verma, 1999). Changing attitudes towards children's safety and their ability to manage risk is an integral aspect of this discussion. As noted, generational trends indicate children's diminishing engagement in outdoor play; some commentators suggest this is influenced to some extent by parental fears for safety and the growing culture of blame and litigation. Parents, popular culture, the media and others express the view that child safety is paramount and efforts to optimise child safety in all circumstances is in the best interests of the child. Undoubtedly, injury prevention plays a key role in promoting safety. However, increased parental anxiety about safety that results in increased childhood surveillance and restriction of independent movement may in fact be doing more harm in the long term. Children and young people need challenge and varied stimulation in order to develop normal risk assessment and risk management strategies. Play facilities that offer no challenge become boring, leading children to seek excitement elsewhere, often at much greater danger to themselves and others. Eager and Little (2008) describe a risk and play-deprived child as being more prone to problems such as obesity, mental health concerns, lack of independence, and a decrease in learning, perception and judgement skills. Such conditions are exacerbated when risk is removed from play and restrictions are set too high by adults.

The role of play

Play acts across several adaptive systems to promote enhanced health, well-being and resourcefulness. Emerging fields of research are helping us better understand the role and function of play in the context of establishing an interrelationship and interplay between genes, brain, body, behaviour and the physical and social environment (Lester and Russell, 2008). This deeper understanding and appreciation of how play contributes to children and young people's physical and emotional well-being and to their development is fascinating. Play has a constructive and instructive impact on the architectural foundations of development, such as gene expression and the physical and chemical development of the brain. The same foundations influence our ability to adapt, survive and thrive in social and physical environments. Adolescent play therefore provides rich opportunities for socialisation, informal learning and the practice of critical life skills, such as negotiation, listening, taking turns, conducting relationships, dealing with conflict, considering the opinion of others and managing risk (Crandall, Nolan and Morgan, 1980).

The YLT survey findings, aligned with other studies conducted with and by children, have assisted our understanding of what, in the words of these players, constitutes quality leisure time experience. Consistent with the findings of Hendry et al. (1993) the 2010 YLT survey confirms that adolescent play is varied, ranging from 'fixed play sites' to simply 'hanging out' and being with friends, to more casual activities (such as skateboarding or surfing the internet), to more formal structured activities (such as organised sports, arts or music groups). Adolescents seek places to go that best reflect their social and cultural lives, whether it is congregating in public space, or socialising by simply hanging out with their friends in their neighbourhood. It must be understood that planning for play in adolescent years is much more than the local council providing a quick fix youth shelter or fencing off areas for ball games. As one YLT respondent said:

There should be sheltered areas for young people to hang out in during evening times, play parks for older children such as 14+ without supervision, just a sheltered area where teens can hang out and parents know where it is.

The YLT survey shows that young people themselves are acutely aware of the importance of play for their lives. Eighty per cent of 16 year olds agreed with the statement that 'young people who have no space or time to play will not develop into healthy adults'. Almost all respondents (97%) agreed that 'every child and young person should have easy access to public spaces for play and leisure', and nearly two thirds (64%) disagreed with the statement that 'playing is just something for younger children'.

The YLT evidence supports the fact that screen-based and social media play is on the rise: survey results highlight that 65 per cent of 16 year olds in Northern Ireland spend time every day on some form of screen-based activity. According to Valkenburg, Schouten and Peter (2005) children are increasingly developing virtual spaces and online identities through the use of media

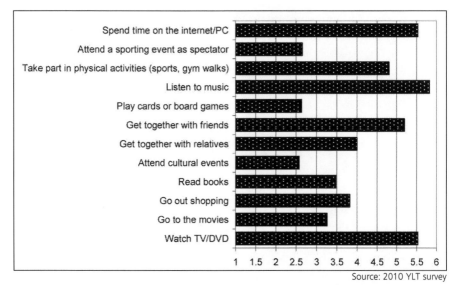

Source: 2010 YLT survey

Figure 5.2 Average frequency* with which respondents are involved in the following leisure time activities (mean scores)

*Meaning of scores: 6 = 'Daily', 5 = 'Several times a week', 4 = 'Several times a month', 3 = 'Several times a year', 2 = 'Less often', 1 = 'Never'.

technology. In the YLT survey, playing computer games, watching TV and listening to music were the three most frequently undertaken leisure time activities (see Figure 5.2). Females and males were equally likely to spend their leisure time watching TV or videos or to spend it in front of the computer. However, 16 year olds from poorer backgrounds spent significantly less time on the computer or on the internet. The frequency and impact of social media and screen based technology is becoming an area of health and safety concern for many commentators.

As discussed by Lester and Russell (2008) in *Play for a Change*, children and young people's use of media technologies represents complex and multiple contradictions for adults. On the one hand, we value our children being 'safe' indoors, yet at the same time there are anxieties and tensions about what children actually get up to, and about their safety online (Crowe and Bradford, 2006). Much of the research into children's media use is criticised for adopting highly generalised approaches and failing to take into account the specific social, economic and cultural context for use of new technologies by children. The contradictions and confusions are compounded by conflicting results from studies into the harm or benefit of game play (Buckingham, 2000). There are increasing concerns and 'moral panics' about the risks to health and safety whilst engaged in gaming, social media and screen-based activity (Gentile *et al.*, 2004). Many studies highlight the harmful impact of playing violent computer games, citing increased levels of violence and aggression, decreased academic success and poorer social and emotional maturity. Equally, other studies would suggest exactly the opposite, suggesting new technologies enable children and young people to establish strong peer communities and become rich social agents in their daily lives (Schott and Hodgetts, 2006).

Policy agenda for play

Central government interest in children's play and the wider social world of children has been a mixed bag over successive parliaments under different political parties; but on the whole play has not been taken particularly seriously at Westminster. In more recent years however, a number of related agendas have come together, and concerns over childhood obesity and healthy lifestyles, concerns over crime and anti-social behaviour, the introduction of more universal childcare, and the growth in early years education have all contributed to raising the profile of play in the lives of children. Steadily the social policy context for children's play across the UK has been changing. The Play Sector has contributed to the discussion and has been increasingly effective in getting play on to the social policy agenda. Research and campaigning by play organisations across the UK have successfully drawn government attention to the need for a more strategic approach to play, by helping government to consider play in a much broader context than they might otherwise have done.

In 2002 the culmination of collective advocacy resulted in significant Big Lottery investment in play, with £200 million of Lottery funds made available across the UK with the aim of creating children's play opportunities nationally by improving and developing inclusive play provision in areas of greatest need. The funding further encouraged the first ever government-sponsored review of children's play in the UK. Commissioned by the Department for Culture, Media and Sport and the Department for Education and Skills, with support from the Big Lottery, other government departments and the administrations of Wales, Scotland and Northern Ireland, the review was headed up, and chaired by the Rt Hon Frank Dobson.

The report *Getting Serious about Play: A Review of Children's Play* (Dobson, 2004) – also known as the *Dobson Review* – led to recommendations on the use of lottery funding through a UK-wide dedicated play programme. An outworking of this was the formation of England's first national Play Strategy. Under the Labour Government, the Strategy set out a vision and established a commitment to achieving better play opportunities in England. As well as focusing on the specific places where children play, like parks and green spaces, schools and children's centres, the Play Strategy also considered how communities and neighbourhoods could become more welcoming and child-friendly.

In recent years, the devolved administrations in Scotland, Wales and Northern Ireland have also contributed to the policy framework, each having developed specific policy for play in the home nations. The national play organisations, with varying degrees of success, continue to contribute and lead the debate; the net result of this collective approach is serious interest in play now being shown by legislators at national and home nation levels across the UK. One of the more interesting and most recent developments is that of the approach being taken by the Welsh Assembly. In May 2013 a Play Sufficiency Statutory Duty was established requiring all local authorities to assess, monitor and ultimately invest in the sufficiency of play opportunities for all children within council boundaries. Wales is the first country in the world to have this duty, and so we are eagerly watching their progress. Perhaps this is something that the other jurisdictions should be aspiring to achieve.

Local policy perspective

In the context of local policy development, PlayBoard has been working closely with the Northern Ireland Executive since 2005 on the development of a policy framework for play. This endeavour culminated in the Northern Ireland Executive publishing both a policy statement for play and an accompanying implementation plan (OFMDFM, 2009, 2011).

As previously noted, across the western world important changes are framing the social structures and processes that shape our children's lives (James and James, 2004). Northern Ireland is no different in that social, technological and environmental changes and children's rights advancements are transforming the political and environmental context wherever children are growing up. In the last decade there has been increasing recognition of the importance of play and a growing appreciation that government and other public bodies have a responsibility to create the conditions for play to occur. The impetus for the development of a policy statement on play in Northern Ireland was predicated by a number of key drivers:

- The UNCRC (1989) – Article 31 of the Convention established play as a specific right and entitlement in childhood.
- UNCRC commentary, wherein concern was noted in States Party reviews. It was highlighted that in Northern Ireland there was poor recognition, implementation and investment in Article 31 rights.
- The establishment of the Office of the Northern Ireland Commissioner for Children and Young People (NICCY). Research conducted on behalf of the Commissioner's office in 2004 – *Children's Rights in Northern Ireland* – identified play and leisure as key areas of concern by children and by parents (Kilkelly et al., 2004).
- Development of a Children's Strategy for Northern Ireland *Our Children and Young People, Our Pledge* (OFMDFM, 2006). Consultation on the Strategy again identified play and leisure as key areas for development. One of the high level outcomes (Enjoying, Learning and Achieving) further identified the development of a play policy as a tangible action.

The Northern Ireland play policy journey commenced in October 2005, when it was announced that the Northern Ireland Assembly was minded to develop a policy statement for play. PlayBoard was invited to assist officials in developing a public consultation document on a draft policy statement. Subsequently, following a long gestation and several public consultations, the Office of the First Minister and Deputy First Minster as the lead department for Children and Young People on behalf of the Northern Ireland Executive, published Northern Ireland's inaugural Play and Leisure policy statement (OFMDFM, 2009). In recognition that the policy was targeted at all children and young people up to the age of 18, the word 'leisure' was added to the title of the final publication. The final statement's aspirations and narrative were informed, underpinned and founded upon the UNCRC (1989) principles of provision, protection and participation.

The 2009 Play and Leisure Policy statement identifies play and leisure as being 'essential elements' of holistic child development and recognises their centrality in children's and young people's lived experiences. The final statement discusses the importance of play and leisure for happy fulfilled childhoods, whilst also recognising the role of play in supporting family life and promoting community cohesion. The final policy states its aim as 'establishing play within a policy framework that recognises and values play and leisure as a meaningful contribution to society'. Importantly, the policy stresses and supports the view that children and young people have agency and the desire and potential to be active participants in their local communities and society more generally. The development of an implementation framework for the realisation of the play and leisure policy statement was underpinned by the principle of participation. The 2010 YLT survey was one of the multiple consultative approaches that were employed to ensure children and young people's voices and views were factored into every stage of the drafting process. Issues and concerns identified by children and young people include:

- Facilities that are inappropriate for different age groups.
- Limited access to recreational facilities in local communities.
- Cost of leisure time activities.
- Lack of activities for older children.
- Lack of space and place in the public domain.

Many 16 year olds who completed the 2010 YLT survey shared these concerns and experiences. Forty-five per cent of YLT respondents felt that play facilities in their local area were poor or very poor. The lack of access to spaces and places for play and leisure was particularly significant for those living in rural areas and for those with disabilities. The lack of spaces and places for teenagers to hang out and socialise in and the negative attitudes of adults towards young people have already been alluded to above. At the time of writing, in 2013 the issues remain, and will continue to remain as long as the Northern Ireland Executive's play and leisure framework remains unresourced, and stored safely on a departmental shelf.

Discussion and conclusions

This chapter set out to fulfil two purposes: first, to provide a platform for a wider discussion on the subject of play; and second, to provide an overview of the key findings from the YLT survey which offered insights into the play and leisure experiences and desires of young people at the age of 16.

The chapter affirms that children have a wealth of situated knowledge about their environments and about how space, time and attitudes shape their everyday interactions and experiences. Play behaviour may change over time but, as confirmed by the 16 year olds who participated in the YLT survey, the need and desire to play is important. Play is part of the human condition and part of our basic nature; consequently playfulness is a mode of being which spurs our inquisitive nature throughout the entire life span. Play is not just about destination-fixed play sites; it is about experimentation, manipulation and investigation. Play aids our own personal journey of discovery and learning.

Barriers

Numerous surveys, local, national and international, highlight that parents and children alike want more and better opportunities and they want safe play close to where they live. Yet the YLT survey reveals that there are multiple systemic barriers prohibiting young people's right to play, and their enjoyment of play and leisure opportunities. These issues are exacerbated for children with disabilities, those living in rural areas and for those from migrant communities. YLT notes numerous access difficulties aligned to age, gender, ability, cost and transport. It is no wonder that the evidence suggests a growing penchant for indoor screen-based sedentary activity.

The issue of personal safety in discussions of play is perennial; interestingly, perhaps due to commentary and media exposure, it is an issue identified by parents and children alike. Time and again, personal safety is cited as a significant concern and the singular factor that most prevents children from playing outdoors. Commentators are now taking this subject more seriously and are beginning to highlight that the health and safety agenda may be promoting a culture of overprotection. Injury prevention and fear of 'dangerous strangers' may fundamentally be hindering children's health and well-being. The generational trend of diminishing engagement in outdoor play is affecting children's physical and mental health and promoting a lack of participation in challenging, riskier play pursuits. In turn, this may be affecting independence, perception and essential judgement skills. Ironically, keeping children safe may also involve exposing them to challenge and managed risk. New avenues for investigation and action are emerging seeking optimal strategies for keeping children 'as safe as necessary', not 'as safe as possible'. How do we develop play spaces and experiences that allow children to challenge and push personal boundaries, which provide the exhilaration and thrill that children seek but are still ultimately safe?

Participation in decisions on play and leisure spaces

Participation of children in planning processes is still virtually non-existent. In spite of growing awareness of the need for this and the fact that children have a right to express their views on all matters affecting them and to have those views given due weight, as the YLT survey results show, planning is still done *for* instead of *with* children. Despite the fact that they are the service users, children and young people are regularly excluded from community life and decisions on play and leisure. When asked in the YLT survey about their input in the design of play and leisure services, it was disappointing to note that only two per cent of respondents had been asked for their views. This was despite the fact that 91 per cent of respondents felt that they should be consulted and indeed had interesting insights for improvements that, if taken on board, would in fact benefit the whole community. For example, one young person said:

> *Many buildings close to where I live are becoming increasingly derelict – such buildings could be put to good use . . . creating alternative places for young people to hang about in, rather than those too young to get into bars, resulting in hanging around street corners annoying residents.*

Embedding stakeholder participation as a core principle of community design would perhaps help foster civic ownership and ensure relevancy and added value. Creative and participatory approaches to design and land usage would undoubtedly support better play, leisure and healthier lifestyle choices. Designers and planners need to consider children's rights and expressed wishes to be consulted and involved in the development of attractive, exciting and welcoming places. Adopting a collaborative approach with the players and their parents may offer an agreeable solution and in due course foster the conditions that will empower parental confidence to let their children outside to play.

Negative attitudes towards children and young people

This chapter also picked up on the fact that children's lives have changed in dramatic ways in recent years. Important changes in the social structures and processes that help shape children's lives have fuelled a viewpoint, which suggests our children are encountering wider ranging societal opportunities than their contemporaries of previous generations. However, the YLT survey findings present a bit of a paradox. Despite the narrative on greater self-determination, the findings highlight that young people are encountering numerous societal constraints and significant barriers in relation to their experiences of play and leisure. Take for example the extent to which young people are experiencing negativity in their local communities; 56 per cent of YLT respondents reported that they had been moved on in the community simply for playing in the street or hanging out with friends, 85 per cent reported that they felt they have been judged negatively simply for being young, and 79 per cent indicated they felt the media compounded the situation by portraying young people negatively. In some quarters of society, children simply playing out in the community are deemed to be antisocial and unsavoury. Issues identified in this chapter highlight that young people feel they are disrespected, disadvantaged and disaffected by virtue of simply being young. It is of interest that this matter has also been consistently raised by the UNCRC in States Parties commentary, with the most recent one in 2008 stipulating that the UK State Party needed to take immediate action to reduce the negative portrayal of young people.

Public profiling and celebrating the positive contribution of our children and young people may provide a counter-balance and help dispel some of the societally-held negative attitudes. Children and young people are an asset that should be viewed and treated as valuable and active participants in their communities rather than passive recipients of socialisation, regulation and control.

The way forward

Children's lives are complex. If we are to succeed with creating child friendly and play-friendly communities then the multiple and complex variables undoubtedly require progressive mutual accommodation. There are often many different, divergent and contradictory explanations for the nature and value of play. As stated by Brian Sutton-Smith in the opening chapter of his book *The Ambiguity of Play*, when we come to discuss play or make theoretical statements about its benefits we find 'there is little agreement among us and much ambiguity' (2001: 1). Within this context there is a compelling need to continue to connect research, practice and policy. Success, at whatever level, policy or operational, requires the co-operation of many different professionals and individuals. We each have a role to play in affecting change: elected representatives; council officers; teachers; children's services professionals; planners; developers; architects; housing managers; landscape architects; designers; play equipment suppliers; parks and recreation managers; community groups; health professionals, play practitioners and, it goes without saying, parents are just some of the people who have, or *should have*, an interest in promoting enjoyable play spaces that feel safe and welcoming to children and young people. We need to work at fostering a genuine collaborative approach, share resources and agree priorities for action around play. Localised play strategies can be adopted and firmly embedded within the wider top-tier plans and strategies for our cities and council areas. If we are to create joined-up children's services and child-friendly environments that genuinely place children at the heart of their communities, play needs to be aligned with and coordinated within an overall vision for children and young people which is expressed in policy and strategy.

Finally, children and young people have a fundamental right and entitlement to engage in play (UNCRC, 1989). As the new General Comment (GC-17) on Article 31 points out, States Parties and devolved administrations need to adopt a more strategic approach to play and leisure provision. Such strategic frameworks need to offer co-ordinated guidance, standards and direction. This chapter alludes to the fact that policy on play is piecemeal and furthermore play appears to remain a low priority. The Northern Ireland Executive need to show leadership and deliver on the aspirations and actions contained in their established play and leisure policy framework. The UNCRC is clear: no regressive measures in respect of Article 31 are permitted. While the Convention provides for what it terms 'progressive realisation' of economic, social and cultural rights, and whilst it recognises the problems arising from limited resources, it imposes on States Parties the specific and continuing obligation, even when resources are inadequate, to 'strive to ensure the widest possible enjoyment of the relevant rights under the prevailing circumstances'. When is our Executive going to take decisive action? They need to move beyond listening into a hearing mode.

To reiterate, the benefits of investing in play and leisure are long-term; however, we need action in the short term if we are to realise our children's optimal development. Children and young people's happiness and well-being requires them to play in the *here and now*, and if enabled to do so society will reap the dividends as today's children are tomorrow's creative thinkers, innovators and ultimate decision makers.

References

Beckett, H. (2010) Adolescents' Experiences of the Right to Play and Leisure in Northern Ireland. *Childcare in Practice*, 16: 3, 227–40.

Beunderman, J., Hannon, C. and Bradwell, P. (2007) *Seen and Heard: Reclaiming the Public Realm With Children and Young People*. London: Demos.

Buckingham, D. (2000) *After the Death of Childhood: Growing up in The Age of Electronic Media*. Cambridge: Polity Press.

CRC-C-GC-17 (2013) *The Right of the Child to Rest, Leisure, Play, Recreational Activities, Cultural Life and The Arts (Article 31)*. Geneva: United Nations Office of the High Commissioner for Human Rights. Accessed Sept. 2013 at: www2.ohchr.org/english/bodies/crc/docs/GC/CRC-C-GC-17_en.doc

Crandall, R., Nolan, M. and Morgan, L. (1980) Leisure and Social Interaction. In: Iso-Ahola, S.E. (Ed.) *Social Psychological Perspectives on Leisure and Recreation*. Dubuque, IA: Wm. C. Brown.

Crowe, N. and Bradford, S. (2006) Hanging out in Runescape: Identity, Work and Leisure in the Virtual Playground. *Children's Geographies*, 4: 3, 331–46.

Dobson, F. (2004) *Getting Serious About Play: A Review of Children's Play.* London: Department for Culture.

Eager, D. and Little, H. (2008) *Children Need Risk*, 17th International Play Association World Conference, Hong Kong, 8–11 January.

Ellis, M.J. (1973) *Why People Play.* New Jersey: Prentice Hall.

Gentile, G.A., Lynch, P.L., Linder, J.R. and Walsh, D.A. (2004) The Effects of Violent Video Game Habits on Adolescent Hostility, Aggressive Behaviours and School Performance. *Journal of Adolescence*, 27: 1, 5–22.

Gill, T. (2007) *No Fear: Growing up in a Risk Adverse Society.* London: Calouste Gulbenkian Foundation.

Gladwin, M. and Collins, J. (2008) *Anxieties and Risks.* In: Collins, J. and Foley, P. (Eds.) *Promoting Children's Wellbeing: Policy and Practice.* Bristol: Policy Press.

Hendry, L.B. et al. (1993) *Young People's Leisure and Lifestyles.* London: Routledge.

Hughes, B. (2003) Play Deprivation, Play Bias and Playwork Practice. In: Brown, F. (Ed.) *Playwork Theory and Practice.* London: Open University Press.

James, A. and James. A. (2004) *Constructing Childhood: Theory, Policy and Social Practice.* Houndmills: Palgrave Macmillan.

Kilkelly, U. et al. (2004) *Children's Rights in Northern Ireland.* Belfast: Northern Ireland Commissioner for Children and Young People.

Larson, R.W. and Verma, S. (1999) How Children and Adolescents Spend Time Around The World: Work, Play and Developmental Opportunities. *Psychological Bulletin*, 125: 6, 701–36.

Lester, S. and Russell, W. (2008) *Play for a Change – Play, Policy and Practice: A Review of Contemporary Perspectives* (Summary Report). London: Play England.

Lester, S. and Russell, W. (2010) *Children's Right to Play: An Examination of The Importance of Play in The Lives of Children Worldwide.* The Hague: Bernard van Leer Foundation.

Levy, J. (1978) *Play Behavior.* Florida: John Wiley and Sons.

Madge, N. (2006) *Children These Days.* Bristol: The Policy Press.

Madge, N. and Baker, J. (2007) *Risk and Childhood.* London: The Royal Society for the Encouragement of Arts, Manufactures and Commerce.

McAlister, S., Scraton, P. and Haydon, D. (2010) 'Insiders' and 'Outsiders': young people, place and identity in Northern Ireland. *Shared Space*, 9: 68–83.

Moyles, J.R. (1989) *Just Playing? The Role and Status of Play in Early Childhood Education.* Maidenhead: Open University Press.

NICCY (2008) *Children's Rights: Rhetoric or Reality A Review of Children's Rights in Northern Ireland 2007/2008*, Belfast: Northern Ireland Commissioner for Children and Young People.

OFMDFM (Office of the First Minister and Deputy First Minister) (2006) *Our Children and Young People – Our Pledge: A Ten-Year Strategy For Children and Young People in Northern Ireland 2006–2016.* Belfast: OFMDFM.

OFMDFM (2009) *Play and Leisure Policy.* Belfast: OFMDFM.

O'Loughlin, J., Stevenson, B. and Schubotz, D. (2011) *Playscapes at 16*, ARK Research Update 74, Belfast: ARK. Accessed 15.09.2013 at: www.ark.ac.uk/publications/updates/update74.pdf

Pink, D.H. (2009) *Drive: The Surprising Truth About What Motivates Us.* New York: Riverhead Books.

Rennie, S. (2003) Making Play Work: The Fundamental Role of Play in The Development of Social Relationships. In: Brown, F. (Ed.) *Playwork: Theory and Practice*. Open University Press.

Schott, G. and Hodgetts, D. (2006) Health and Digital Gaming. *Journal of Health Psychology,* 11: 2, 309–16.

Schubotz, D. and McCooey, R. (2013) *PlayScapes at 16: Revisited*. Belfast: PlayBoard.

Sutton-Smith, B. (2001) *The Ambiguity of Play*. Cambridge: Harvard University Press.

UNCRC (United Nations Convention on the Rights of the Child) (1989) Geneva: United Nations Office of the High Commissioner for Human Rights. Accessed Sept. 2013 at: www.ohchr.org.

Valkenburg, P., Schouten, A. and Peter, J. (2005) Adolescents Identity Experiments on the Internet. *New Media and Society*, 7: 3, 383–402.

WHO (World Health Organization) (2002) *The World Health Report 2002: Reducing Risk, Promoting Health*. Geneva: WHO.

CHAPTER 6

Sexual Exploitation and Sexual Violence in Adolescence

Helen Beckett

Introduction

This chapter considers the issue of sexual exploitation and sexual violence in adolescence through a safeguarding lens. Conceptualising the issue as a safeguarding concern in this manner is not about denying the rights or agency of young people. Nor is it about denying or policing adolescent sexuality, as has too often been the case in Northern Ireland to date. It is however, about recognising that adolescents, even those who can legally consent to have sex, can also be victims of abuse where their experience of sexual activity occurs without freely given consent, where it is tied up in an exchange transaction, or where there is a clear power differential at play. On this basis, it is also about highlighting the need to:

- Be open to talking to young people about sex, consent, power and abuse.
- Educate young people about healthy relationships.
- Equip young people, parents, carers and professionals to identify exploitative or abusive relationships where they do occur.
- Provide appropriate support and intervention when required.

Although the primary operational focus of safeguarding structures within Northern Ireland, and indeed across the United Kingdom, has historically been that of risks to younger children (particularly in the post 'Baby P' climate) we are recently beginning to see an increasing recognition of the need to actively protect adolescents from a range of safeguarding concerns, not least of which are those associated with sexual exploitation and sexual violence. A number of inter-related factors have contributed to this emerging acknowledgment of adolescent risk. These include a number of high profile group sexual exploitation cases in England, the serious case reviews that have accompanied them and an increasing body of research evidence on sexual exploitation and sexual violence in adolescence and consequent increased policy discourse on the issue.

To date, England has led the way within the United Kingdom in terms of policy activity around sexual exploitation. Pertinent outputs include the publication of specific guidance on child sexual exploitation (DCSF, 2009) followed by an action plan (DfE, 2011) step-by-step guide for practitioners (DfE, 2012) and a series of guidance documents for local authorities (Barnardo's and Local Government Association, 2012; Local Government Association, 2013). However, Scotland, Wales and Northern Ireland are also now engaging in more active policy discourse around the issue.

Within Northern Ireland specifically, research conducted by the author on behalf of Barnardo's Northern Ireland (Beckett, 2011) raised the profile of sexual exploitation amongst both practitioners and policy makers. Following this, the newly established Safeguarding Board for Northern Ireland (SBNI) – the body with the legislative remit for overseeing safeguarding within Northern Ireland – has proposed a priority focus on the connected issues of child sexual exploitation, missing persons and e-safety in their first strategic plan for 2013–16 (SBNI, 2013). The Association of Chief Police Officers has also recently issued a UK-wide Child Sexual Exploitation Action Plan (ACPO, 2012), which the Police Service for Northern Ireland (PSNI) are taking forward. In light of these, and other concurrent developments, the issue of sexual exploitation and sexual violence in adolescence is gaining increasing currency as a safeguarding concern within Northern Ireland, with significant changes in policy and practice discourse and implementation anticipated in the next few years. As explored throughout this chapter, the findings of the sexual exploitation module in the 2010 Young Life and Times (YLT) survey, and the wider Barnardo's sexual exploitation research that it was part of, offer vital insights for taking this work forward.

Sexual exploitation and sexual violence in adolescence

Child sexual exploitation is a form of child sexual abuse that predominantly, although not exclusively, impacts upon adolescents, with the average age at which concerns first come to the attention of agencies being between 13 and 15 years of age (Barnardo's, 2011, 2012; Beckett, 2011; OCC, 2012). Both males and females are known to be sexually exploited, but studies repeatedly identify significantly higher proportions of identified concerns amongst females (at least four times that of males). It is, however, important to note that this variation in identification does not necessarily equate with such a significant variation in experience, as lower levels of awareness of risk for young males and lower levels of reporting by male victims are likely to disguise the true extent of exploitation amongst young males (Palmer, 2001; Harper and Scott,

2006; Barnardo's, 2011; Beckett, 2011; CEOP, 2011; Jago et al., 2011; Brodie, 2012).

Developed from the now passé concept of 'child prostitution', the term child sexual exploitation is understood to involve:

> *Exploitative situations, contexts and relationships where young people (or a third person or persons) receive 'something' (e.g. food, accommodation, drugs, alcohol, cigarettes, affection, gifts, money) as a result of them performing, and/or another or others performing on them, sexual activities . . . In all cases, those exploiting the child/young person have power over them by virtue of their age, gender, intellect, physical strength and/or economic or other resources. Violence, coercion and intimidation are common, involvement in exploitative relationships being character-ised in the main by the child or young person's limited availability of choice, resulting from their social/economic and/or emotional vulnerability.*

(DCSF, 2009: 9)

As can be seen from the above definition, sexual exploitation is an umbrella term that incorporates a wide range of scenarios. The 2011 study conducted on behalf of Barnardo's identified three particular types of sexual exploitation as particularly prevalent within Northern Ireland:

- *Abuse through prostitution*: Part Three of the Sexual Offences (NI) Order 2008 clearly stipulates that it is an offence to abuse any child under the age of 18 years through prostitution. This includes intentionally paying for the sexual services of a child and inciting, arranging or controlling this in any manner. Although often misunderstood to only include 'sex for money', the offence of abuse through prostitution is actually much broader than that, including the provision of goods or services (including drugs or alcohol) at a reduced cost, or the discharge of a debt, in return for sexual activity. Although very few cases of this nature are recorded within criminal justice statistics, the 2011 research clearly identified it to be an issue of serious concern, both in terms of an individual paying for the sexual services of a child and a third party arranging or controlling this.
- *The 'party house' model*: The typical party house scenario involves an abuser or abusers building up a relationship with a young person, bringing them along to parties with 'free' access to drugs and alcohol, and at some stage collecting on their 'investment' through enforced or coerced sexual activity with themselves or others. The party scenario shares many similarities with the abuse of a child through prostitution, but in these cases, the exchange is generally less apparent upfront, with 'payment' or 'trade off' demanded or forcefully taken retrospectively.

- *Sexually exploitative relationships*: These 'relationships' generally involve young people under the legal age of consent in, what they perceive to be, a consensual sexual relationship with their boy or girlfriend, 10, 20 or even 30 years their senior. While an age gap in a relationship does not necessarily indicate exploitation, where the young person is under the legal age of consent and the age gap is substantial it is hard to conceive how such a situation would not be exploitative (Beckett, 2011).

Internet exploitation, child abuse images and trafficking for the purposes of sexual exploitation were also identified as significant issues of concern in Northern Ireland, although less frequently so than the three types cited above in the Barnardo's research.

The examples of sexual exploitation identified in the wider research were variably perpetrated by individuals, informal networks of abusers or organised groups. Although sexual exploitation is often commonly understood to involve adult perpetrators and child victims, both the YLT study and the wider research also revealed a significant issue of peer-on-peer exploitation with almost one quarter (24%) of identified sexual exploitation cases in the wider study involving adolescent perpetrators.

As explored in greater depth later in the chapter, the YLT survey also identified the wider, but closely related, matter of sexual violence to be a significant issue for adolescents in Northern Ireland. Utilising the definition provided within the Regional Sexual Violence Strategy, the term sexual violence can be understood to encompass 'any behaviour perceived to be of a sexual nature which is unwanted or takes place without consent or understanding' (NIO and DHSSPS, 2008). Although sharing many similarities with cases of sexual exploitation in terms of a power differential and the exploitative nature of the act, the absence of an exchange transaction places such cases outside of the definitional parameters of sexual exploitation.

The identification of serious concerns about sexual violence in adolescence, particularly that occurring within a peer-on-peer context, mirrors findings from a wide range of other recent studies within the United Kingdom (Maxwell, 2006; Barter et al., 2009; Maxwell and Aggleton, 2009; Firmin, 2010; Barter, 2011; Beckett, 2011; Coy, Thiara and Kelly, 2011; Beckett et al., 2012; OCC, 2012; Schubotz, 2012). A survey of 1,353 13 to17 year olds in England, Scotland and Wales, for example, identified violence in young people's intimate relationships to be a 'significant child welfare problem', particularly for young women. This included sexual violence, with one in six boys and one in three girls aged 13 to 17 years saying that they had experienced some form of sexual partner violence (Barter et al., 2009).

Existing studies on peer sexual violence and exploitation importantly highlight the wider context of gendered power relationships and a deeply-rooted notion amongst many young people (of both genders) that girls' bodies are somehow the property of boys. They also highlight the impact of exposure to pornography on young people's sexual beliefs, significant confusion around issues of consent, and a lack of clarity amongst adolescents as to what constitutes healthy relationships and healthy sexuality, all of which are equally pertinent within Northern Ireland (Maxwell and Aggleton, 2009; Firmin, 2010; Coy, Thiara and Kelly, 2011; Ringrose et al., 2012, Beckett et al., 2012; Horvath et al., 2013).

Legislative and policy context

Whilst there is no specific offence of sexual exploitation or sexual violence *per se* in the case of children and young people, Part Three of the Sexual Offences (NI) Order 2008 provides for a wide range of offences relevant to cases of sexual exploitation and sexual violence in adolescence including:

- Rape and other offences against children under 13 (Articles 12 to 15).
- Sexual offences against children under 16 (Articles 16 to 22).
- Sexual offences against children committed by children or young persons (Article 20).
- Abuse of a position of trust, against children under 18 (Articles 23 to 31).
- Familial sex offences against children under 18 (Articles 32 to 36).
- Abuse of children under 18 through prostitution and pornography (Articles 37 to 41).
- Indecent photographs of children under 18 (Article 42).

The stipulations of the Order make it clear that the granting of consent by a child under 16 years of age is immaterial to whether or not a sexual offence has taken place, given that the child cannot legally offer this consent. The Order also addresses the issue of 'mistaken age', clarifying that this is irrelevant in the case of any child under the age of 13, but maintaining it as a possible defence in cases where the victim is 13 to 15 years of age. Whilst the legal age of consent is established at 16 years of age, the Order recognises that 16/17 year olds still require protection in certain circumstances, including those of familial sexual offences, abuse of a position of trust, abuse through prostitution, and pornography and child abuse images.

The law also provides for a number of civil remedies that can be used in cases of sexual exploitation, including Sexual Offences Prevention Orders (SOPOs) available post conviction of a sexual offence and Risk of Sexual Harm Orders (RSHOs) available for use in the absence of a conviction. Article 69 of the Children (NI) Order 1995 and Article 4 of the Child Abduction (NI) Order 1985 can also be utilised where children are going missing as part of their exploitation.

Unlike England and Wales, Northern Ireland does not yet have dedicated guidance on protecting children and young people from sexual exploitation. In the absence of such guidance, the principles and procedures that underpin current responses to sexual exploitation are drawn from safeguarding documents introduced almost ten years ago when knowledge about the issue was much more limited than it is now (DHSSPS, 2003; HSSB, PSNI and NSPCC, 2004; ACPCs, 2005). While these documents outline a number of important principles for addressing sexual exploitation – recognition as a form of sexual abuse; multi-agency responsibility; the primacy of the welfare of the child; the need for support and effective rehabilitation of victims; and a responsibility to investigate and prosecute perpetrators – they do so within a narrower definition of sexual exploitation than that currently governing responses in England and Wales. As such, the current statutory categorisation of sexual exploitation fails to incorporate the full range of sexually exploitative experiences identified in research or the range of relevant offences recognised in the Sexual Offences (NI) Order 2008, as outlined above. Policy guidance on sexual exploitation is also inadequately situated in relation to other pertinent policies such as the Regional Sexual Violence Strategy (NIO and DHSSPS, 2008) the Working Arrangements for the Welfare and Safeguarding of Child Victims of Human Trafficking (DHSSPS and PSNI, 2011) or the Regional Missing Guidance (HSC Board and PSNI, 2009). It is however hoped that the revision of key safeguarding documents that is currently underway will both better streamline policy articulation in this field and incorporate a more comprehensive and nuanced conceptualisation of sexual exploitation and associated risks in adolescence.

Adolescent sexuality in Northern Ireland

Before exploring the findings of the 2010 YLT survey, it is worth pausing briefly to consider what is known about adolescent sexuality in Northern Ireland more generally. With a few noted exceptions outlined below, studies focusing on the sexual experiences of adolescents in Northern Ireland have focused primarily on patterns of sexual interaction (particularly first sexual experiences) rather than the nature of these interactions. These studies tell us that one quarter of young people in Northern Ireland have had sexual intercourse under the age of 16, with reported rates ranging from 22 to 27 per cent (Schubotz, Simpson and Rolston, 2002; Blake, 2008; Schubotz, 2012). The most common age of first intercourse is reported to range from 13 to 15 years of age (Schubotz, Rolston and Simpson, et al., 2004; Love for Life, 2005; North and West Health Action Zone, 2007; NISRA, 2008, 2010).

Although most young people report being happy with the age of first intercourse in these studies, one in eight females and one in fourteen males who completed the 2011 YLT survey said that they didn't feel ready to have sex but went along with what the other person wanted. Similarly, ten per cent of females (compared to one per cent of males) said that they didn't really want to have sex but felt they should or that they were forced into it (Schubotz, 2012). Alcohol, and to a lesser degree drugs, feature significantly in many young people's reported initial sexual experiences, with between 21 and 43 per cent of young people reporting that they were drunk when they first had sex, and between one and ten percent having taken drugs at that time (Schubotz, Simpson and Rolston, 2002; Schubotz, 2012).

The YLT study

The sexual exploitation module of the 2010 YLT survey asked respondents about their experiences of a range of exploitative sexual experiences, namely:

- Experience of grooming by adults.
- Being taken advantage of sexually when under the influence of alcohol, solvents or drugs.
- Sexual activity in exchange for something.
- Sexual activity under threat.

What is particularly helpful about the survey findings is that they are self reported and collated in anonymous form. Many other studies of sexual exploitation rely on professionals' identification of concerns which, given the low levels of disclosure and variable levels of awareness, are only ever going to represent a partial account of the issue. Where the limitations of the survey arise are in relation to the contextual information about the experiences shared and the relevant parties' perceptions of the interactions described; therefore, where pertinent, this is elucidated with findings from the wider study.

Experiences of sexual grooming

The process of sexual grooming is central to many cases of sexual exploitation. Whilst the process of grooming is not an offence in and of itself, the Sexual Offences (NI) Order 2008 contains a specific offence of meeting (or actioning an intention to meet) a child following sexual grooming. As the Explanatory Guidance to the Order explains 'the article is intended to cover situations where an adult establishes contact with a child and gains the child's trust so that he can arrange to meet the child for the purpose of committing a "relevant offence" against the child' (NIO, 2008: 14).

Providing young people with the following definition of sexual grooming, respondents were asked if they thought any adult had ever tried to groom them.

> *Grooming is when someone tries to build a relationship with or gain the trust of a young person with the aim of getting them to take part in some kind of sexual activity, such as sending or viewing sexual images, sexual conversations or some kind of sexual touching. The relationship will usually appear friendly and harmless at first, because of the clever tricks used to gain the young person's trust but eventually the person will ask, or even pressure, the young person to take part in some kind of sexual activity.*

One in nine respondents (11%) reported such attempted grooming by an adult. Whilst just over half of these young people stated that they had only one such experience, 45 per cent said this had happened to them two or more times. Considering the age at which they had first experienced these grooming attempts, three quarters of those who had experience of this stated that it first happened to them when they were under the legal age of consent (i.e. 16 years of age). Respondents who had experienced more than one attempt at grooming by an adult were asked to answer this and subsequent questions with reference to their first experience of this. One in six said that they were aged 12 years or younger when an adult first tried to groom them.

In virtually all cases (94%) where the gender of the groomer was known, this individual was male. Only five young people (all opposite-sex attracted males) reported experience of a female trying to groom them, although as was the case in the example below, cases of females grooming females were also identified within the wider Barnardo's study:

> *There is a case of a madam, and it's a mix of residential children and local community children that she's exploiting. She uses alcohol and drugs as a route in (Criminal justice representative).*

(Beckett, 2011: 70)

Within YLT, the vast majority (85%) of reported experiences of grooming came from female respondents, with only 15 per cent percent coming from males. This equates to a prevalence rate of one in seven (15%) females, compared to one in 23 males (4%). Differential rates of grooming were also identified on the basis of sexual orientation (23% of same-sex attracted respondents compared to 11 per cent of opposite-sex attracted respondents); disability or illness (21% compared to 10% with no such reported disability/illness); and socio-economic status (17% of respondents who identified themselves as 'not at all' or 'not very well off' reported experience of an adult trying to groom them, compared to 12 per cent of those who described themselves as 'average' and only five per cent of those who described themselves as 'well off' or 'very well off').

Given the almost exclusive focus on internet risk and internet grooming in recent years, it is particularly interesting to note that just over one quarter (28%) of the grooming cases identified in the YLT survey emanated in the online world. The majority (72%) of respondents with experiences of grooming said that they were first approached in person, most frequently when hanging around in communities/on the street, at a pub or club, or through a friend or sibling (see Figure 6.1).

Respondents were also asked to share the outcomes of their experiences of sexual grooming. It is reassuring to note that almost two thirds (63%) said that they didn't engage in any form of sexual activity as a result of the grooming, either because they refused a request to do something sexual or because they

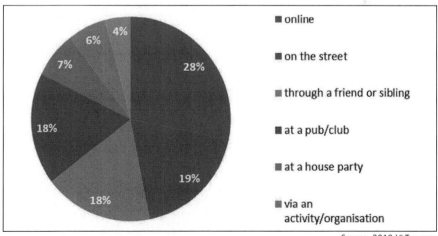

Source: 2010 YLT survey

Figure 6.1   Means of first contact with adult groomer

stopped contact before such a request was made. However, almost one in five (18%) reported that they started a romantic relationship or had some form of face-to-face sexual contact with their groomer. One in eight engaged in sexual texts, emails or conversations with the grooming adult, whilst one in twelve sent or received sexual images.

Interestingly, although greater proportions of females reported experience of an adult trying to groom them, these experiences were more likely to lead to some form of sexual interaction for males; this was especially pronounced in relation to forms of face-to-face sexual contact. Higher proportions of same-sex attracted individuals also reported that they had some form of face-to-face sexual contact with the individual who groomed them compared to their opposite-sex attracted peers.

Sexual activity in exchange for something

The transactional exchange of something tangible in return for sexual activity is perhaps one of the most obvious forms of sexual exploitation and, as noted above, both a distinct offence under the Sexual Offences (NI) Order and a serious issue of concern emerging from the wider research study.

When provided with a list and asked if they had ever been offered any of these things in return for having sex or taking part in any other form of sexual activity, one in twenty respondents reported that they had been offered at least one of these things in return for engaging in some form of sexual activity. Three per cent had been offered drugs, alcohol or solvents; two per cent somewhere to hang out; and two per cent money or other gifts. In the vast majority of these cases (85%) the person who propositioned the young person in this manner was male.

Females were twice as likely to report having been offered something in return for sex/sexual activity (6%) than males (3%). Same-sex attracted respondents reported significantly greater rates than their opposite-sex attracted peers (21% compared to 5%). Economic background also appeared to impact on rates, with almost twice as many of those from 'not-well-off' backgrounds reporting experience of this than those from 'average' or 'well-off' backgrounds (7% compared to 4%), but as with all these categories, the small sample size must be borne in mind when interpreting these figures.

As was the case with grooming, the majority (80%) of respondents who had been offered something in return for sex or other sexual activity were under the legal age of consent when this first happened. What is particularly interesting about the age profile of the victims and perpetrators in these instances is the fact that these cases involved both adult-on-child (54%) and peer-on-peer exploitation (46%). As noted earlier in the chapter, the latter also constitutes sexual exploitation, despite the similar age of the perpetrator and victim, though given the youth of the perpetrator requires a more nuanced response.

Face-to-face first contact with people offering something in return for sexual activity was even more likely to occur than sexual grooming, with only 18 per cent of respondents who had been offered something in return for sex said that this happened online. For the remainder, contact was initiated face-to-face with the most frequent methods of contact being through a friend or sibling (30%), at a house party (24%), hanging around in the community (15%) or at a pub/club (9%).

Experiences of sexual violence when under the influence

As noted earlier on in this chapter, both the YLT survey and the wider Barnardo's research study identified serious concerns about the wider issue of sexual violence in adolescence. A particular concern emerging from the YLT survey was that of being taken advantage of sexually, following the provision of alcohol, solvents or drugs. This was particularly the case for young females, with one in twelve females (8%) reporting experience of this compared to one in 25 males (4%).

Two-thirds (66%) of the young people who reported experiences of this nature said these had first happened to them when they were under 16 years of age, most frequently aged 14 or 15. These incidents tended to be perpetrated more by peers than older adults, with 69 per cent of respondents saying that the person who did this to them was of a similar age (two or fewer years age difference) and only four per cent saying it was by someone five or more years older than them. The following quotations from the wider study illustrate the potential nature of such incidents:

> *Gang type stuff in terms of sexual stuff. Lots of drug taking. Males plying young women with drugs and alcohol and young women off their face in parks at night time and basically the girl being shared if you like and then filmed on mobiles and put on YouTube or Bebo [a social network site] or whatever. That goes on quite a lot. Obviously there is the whole issue of did she consent – she may have at the time but full of blues and vodka, is it informed consent? And did she consent to it being filmed and put on Bebo? And it's always young women from vulnerable backgrounds*

who end up in this situation. We have had seven, eight, nine cases like that in the last six months.

(Criminal justice professional)

They try and make out like it's a big party and you think this is good craic. And then you go to the toilet and they put like a wee sleeper in your drink or a wee E or something in your drink; they'll try and make you drowsy and all. That's what happened to me in [names male]'s house. I kept sayin no to him and he kept puttin tablets in and cos I was blocked I kept lifting the glass and knockin it back. Then I started to feel really sleepy and sick and he was like 'do you want me to put you into bed?' and then I can't remember everything that happened and all I seen was him lying beside me and my jeans was down and all I heard was him saying 'did you enjoy it love?

(Young person) (Beckett, 2011: 53)

As the quotes above aptly illustrate, sexual activity following the provision of substances raises serious questions about consent (defined in the Sexual Offences Order as agreeing by choice, having the freedom and capacity to make that choice) and the prevalence of sexual violence occurring in the absence of free and informed consent.

It is possible, and indeed probable, that the rate of such sexual violence is actually higher than that reported in the YLT survey. This is because the wording of the question only captures those experiences where young people felt they were 'taken advantage of' following the provision of substances. By default this excludes instances where sex took place in situations of question-able consent that the young person does not recall or perceive as having been taking advantage of. Other research clearly shows a vast underestimation of experiences of sexual violence on the basis of a lack of understanding of consent (especially in group scenarios), a lack of understanding of what constitutes sexual activity, and an apparent acceptance of sexual and other forms of violence towards females, on the part of both young women and young men (Barter et al., 2009; Firmin, 2010; Coy, Thiara and Kelly, 2011; Beckett et al., 2012; OCC, 2012). Concerns about these issues relate not only to the impact on the young people at the time, but also the precedent it sets for future relationships and experiences for all parties involved.

Reporting incidences and accessing support

Acknowledging low reporting levels in relation to sexual violence, respondents who reported experience of being offered something in exchange for sexual activity were asked to share if they had ever told a parent or anyone in a position of authority that this had happened to them. Alarmingly, although one fifth had told a friend, almost two thirds (62%) said that they had not reported the incident to a parent or anyone in authority. The wider research study reveals a myriad of reasons why young people do not disclose experiences of sexual violence or exploitation. This can be shame or embarrassment about what has happened, fear of the abuser, the fact that the abuser is providing them with something they need and are unable to get elsewhere (somewhere to stay, a sense of belonging, affection, drugs, money etc.) or a fear that they won't be believed. Reporting rates are also affected by the fact that many young people do not view themselves as victims, or realise they have anything to report. This was observed to be particularly pertinent where the young person believes the abuser to be their boy or girlfriend, where they are getting something tangible in return, or where sexually exploitative experiences are prevalent (and in some instances normalised) amongst their peer group.

Moving forward: the need for awareness raising and education

The findings of the YLT survey and the wider Barnardo's research study offer significant contributions to our understanding of young people's experiences of sexual violence and exploitation. Beyond the fact that they shed light on what has traditionally been a clandestine activity, the breadth of young people who engaged in the survey and the prevalence of sexually exploitative experiences across the heterogeneous population clearly indicate that, whilst patterns of vulnerability may exist, no young person is immune from these risks, whether from adults or their peers. The prevalence of experiences reported within the study, and the help-seeking behaviours associated with them (or absence thereof) also clearly indicate that we have a long way to go if we are to effectively protect children and young people from these exploitative and abusive experiences.

To reiterate what was stated at the beginning, a desire to protect young people from sexual exploitation and sexual violence in adolescence is not about denying their rights, or indeed about denying or policing their sexuality. It is about equipping them to navigate the world of sexuality in a safer, more informed and more empowered manner, and providing them with avenues of support where required. It is also about recognising that adolescents, even those who can legally consent to have sex, can also be victims of abuse where their experience of sexual activity occurs without freely given consent, where it is tied up in an exchange transaction and/or where there is a clear power differential at play.

There is no doubt that sexual exploitation and sexual violence in adolescence are complex and challenging issues to address. Young people's experiences of these are predominantly hidden, often clouded in secrecy, confusion or shame. They are often inextricably linked with many other issues including drug and alcohol use, sexual experimentation, vulnerability or unmet need. They are also undoubtedly shaped by wider societal influences including, but not limited to:

- The failure to mainstream a rights-based discourse around children and young people's lives.
- Discomfort with adolescent sexuality, and indeed the experience of adolescence more generally.
- Deeply rooted patriarchal notions and gendered power relations informing rules around sex, sexuality, masculinity and femininity.
- A historical preoccupation with the 'troubles' that has, and in many ways continues to, overshadow meaningful engagement with critical issues such as these that impact upon children and young people's lives.

Both research and practice evidence clearly articulate the need for a proactive response to sexual exploitation and sexual violence in adolescence. Effectively addressing the issue requires a multi-agency, multi-pronged approach that concurrently addresses the 'three Ps' of prevention, protection and prosecution (Pearce, 2009; CEOP, 2011; Jago et al., 2011; OCC, 2012). It is not practical to offer a full exposition of required improvements within this chapter; this can be found in the report of the wider research study (Beckett, 2011). Instead, it is useful to focus on one particular area of the preventative agenda, that of educative work with young people, highlighting a series of critical learning outcomes that must be delivered in order to begin to develop young people's understanding of, and resilience to, sexual exploitation, sexual violence and associated risks in adolescence.

Whilst the free comments made within the YLT survey positively indicate an understanding of risks within the online world following exposure to awareness raising work within this field, there remains a clear gap in terms of understanding of risk within their offline lives. The focus of preventative work consequently needs to be broadened to incorporate protection in the offline world beyond that traditionally conceptualised as 'stranger danger'. One would think that an obvious mechanism for facilitating this would be Relationships and Sexuality Education (RSE) in schools; however a range of studies have clearly indicated that RSE in Northern Ireland is not relevant to, nor meeting the needs of, many young people in its current form. A number of reasons have been identified for this including:

- The moral/religious perspective incorporated in RSE in Northern Ireland.
- The factual/biological nature of the teaching.
- A bias towards heterosexuality and failure to adequately address issue of homosexuality.

(Fleming, Casson and Reid, n.d; McNamee, 2006; McAlister, Gray and Neill, 2007; North and West Belfast Health Action Zone, 2007, 2008; NICCY, 2009)

The findings of both the YLT survey and the wider study demonstrate that the concepts of healthy/unhealthy relationships, consent, coercion and abuse need to be more explicitly incorporated into RSE and other potential avenues of meaningful dialogue with young people. There is significant work required around young people's expectations of (peer) relationships and their accept-ance of violence and exploitation within these; their confusion around what constitutes consent; their understanding of sexual violence and the relationship between consent and coercion/exploitation. Significant capacity building work is also required in terms of increasing young people's ability to identify risk and their resilience to respond to this. Specific efforts also need to be directed towards the victim-blaming culture that permeated discourse in the free comment section of the survey. These suggest that young women are in some way to blame for their experiences because of how they dress or act, as the following quotes from the two females who completed the 2010 YLT survey show:

> *I understand that there are some innocent people who have to deal with sexual harassment but in most cases it has been the result of the young person doing something stupid e.g. going to a club underage. Making yourself open and easy accessible on the internet or getting involved in the wrong crowd. If you keep yourself safe then it is most likely no-body will bother you.*

> *I would believe that many girls would be targeted on nights out, usually because they are dressed in very little, and it does not help that they are usually drunk. Thankfully not all girls are like this, like my friends and I, but for those who dress badly, I would imagine they're sending out the wrong message and putting themselves at higher risk.*

Though well rehearsed in feminist discourse, this issue is specifically emerging as a significant finding in other studies on adolescent sexual violence in recent years and is one that holds significant implications for the likelihood of disclosing and seeking support (Firmin, 2010; Coy, Thiara and Kelly, 2011; Beckett et al., 2012). Linked to this victim-blaming rhetoric, is a concerning emerging theme amongst adolescents in other recent research by the author that young men, and indeed young women, view a young woman's right to withhold consent to sexual activity as more or less valid dependent upon her perceived prior sexual reputation. A similarly concerning accompanying motif is the assumption that addressing sexual violence is the sole responsibility of young women – teaching them to police their actions, control male behaviours, stand up for themselves and thereby protect themselves – and little to do with young men taking responsibility for their own sexual behaviours (Beckett et al., 2012). Although some of these issues are beginning to be addressed within some schools, the findings of both the YLT survey and the wider research clearly indicate that further work is required. This needs to be undertaken with both males and females, both within the school environment and in more informal settings to ensure inclusion of those outside mainstream education establishments.

The age at which we begin to engage young people in these conversations is another critical factor which must be addressed. Recognising that almost one third of the sexual exploitation cases identified in the wider study were first picked up at the age of 12 or 13, it is vital that children are equipped to identify signs of risk, and know how to protect themselves when faced with these, before this time. In reality, this means commencing this educative work at primary school level, though clearly this should be done by skilled professionals in an age-appropriate manner. This is, of course, likely to be a controversial recommendation to some who feel that children should not be exposed at such things at an early age, but the fact remains that those who would abuse and exploit a child adhere to no such standards and we do a child a serious disservice if we deny this.

To conclude where we began, we need to acknowledge and engage in responding to the fact that it is not only young children who experience sexual abuse, nor only adults who experience sexual violence. Though traditionally overlooked, adolescence is a period that incorporates risks of both, at the hands of adults and peers. In short, we must therefore:

- Be open to talking to young people about sex, consent, power and abuse.
- Educate young people about healthy relationships.
- Equip young people, parents/carers and professionals to identify exploitative or abusive relationships where they do occur.
- Provide appropriate support and intervention when required.

References

ACPCs (Allied Child Protection Consultants) (2005) *Regional Policies and Procedures*. Northern Ireland: ACPCs.

ACPO (Association of Chief Police Officers) (2012) *ACPO Child Sexual Exploitation Action Plan.* England: ACPO.

Barnardo's (2011) *Puppet on a String: The Urgent Need to Cut Children Free From Sexual Exploitation.* Barkingside: Barnardo's.

Barnardo's (2012) *Cutting Them Free: How is the UK Progressing in Protecting Its Children From Sexual Exploitation?* Barkingside: Barnardo's.

Barnardo's and Local Government Association (2012) *Tackling Child Sexual Exploitation: Helping Local Authorities to Develop Effective Responses.* Barkingside: Barnardo's.

Barter, C. (2011) Domestic Violence: Not Just an Adult Problem. *Criminal Justice Matters,* 8: 1, 22–3.

Barter, C. et al. (2009) *Partner Exploitation and Violence in Teenage Intimate Relationships.* London: NSPCC.

Beckett, H. et al. (2012) *Research Into Gang-Associated Sexual Exploitation and Sexual Violence: Interim Report.* Luton: University of Bedfordshire.

Beckett, H. (2011) *Not a World Away: The Sexual Exploitation of Children and Young People in Northern Ireland.* Belfast: Barnardo's NI.

Blake, S. (2008) Honesty About Sex and Relationships: It's Not Too Much to Ask For. In: Schubotz, D. and Devine, P. (Eds.) *Young People in Post-Conflict Northern Ireland. The Past Cannot Be Changed, But The Future Can Be Developed.* Lyme Regis: Russell House Publishing.

Brodie, I. (2012) *Exploring the Scale and Nature of Child Sexual Exploitation in Scotland.* Edinburgh: Scottish Government.

CEOP (Child Exploitation and Online Protection Centre) (2011) *Out of Mind, Out of Sight: Breaking Down The Barriers to Understanding Child Sexual Exploitation.* London: CEOP.

Coy, M., Thiara, R. and Kelly, L. (2011) *Boys Think Girls Are Toys? An Evaluation of the NIA Project Prevention Programme on Sexual Exploitation.* London: London Metropolitan University.

DCSF (Department for Children, Schools and Families) (2009) *Safeguarding Children and Young People From Sexual Exploitation: Supplementary Guidance to Working Together to Safeguard Children.* London: HMSO.

DFE (Department for Education) (2011) *Tackling Child Sexual Exploitation: Action Plan.* London: DFE.

DFE (2012) *What to do if You Suspect a Child is Being Sexually Exploited: A Step by Step Guide For Frontline Practitioners.* London: DFE.

DHSSPS (Department of Health, Social Services and Public Safety) and PSNI (Police Service of Northern Ireland) (2011) *Working Arrangements For The Welfare and Safeguarding of Child Victims of Human Trafficking.* Belfast: DHSSPS.

DHSSPS (2003) *Cooperating to Safeguard Children.* Belfast: DHSSPS.

Firmin, C. (2010) *Female Voice in Violence Project: A Study Into The Impact of Serious Youth and Gang Violence on Women and Girls.* London: Race on the Agenda.

Fleming, P., Casson, K. and Reid, S. (n.d) *An Exploration of Relationships and Sexuality Education in The Southern Area: Summary Report.* Armagh: Southern Health and Social Services Board.

Harper, Z. and Scott, S. (2006) *Meeting the Needs of Sexually Exploited Young People in London.* Barkingside: Barnardo's.

HSC Board and PSNI (2009) *Regional Guidance on Police Involvement in Residential Units/ Safeguarding of Children Missing From Home and Foster Care.* Belfast: DHSSPS.

HSSB (Health and Social Services Board), PSNI (Police Service of Northern Ireland) and NSPCC (2004) *Protocol For Joint Investigation by Social Workers and Police Officers of Alleged and Suspected Cases of Child Abuse*. Belfast: DHSSPS.

Horvath, M.A.H. et al. (2013) *Basically . . . Porn is Everywhere. A Rapid Evidence Assessment on The Effects That Access and Exposure to Pornography Has on Children and Young People*. London: Office of the Children's Commissioner.

Jago, S. et al. (2011) *What's Going on to Safeguard Children and Young People From Sexual Exploitation? How Local Partnerships Respond to Child Sexual Exploitation*. Luton: University of Bedfordshire.

Local Government Association (2013) *How Councils Are Raising Awareness of Child Sexual Exploitation*. London: Local Government Association.

Love for Life (2005) *Risk Behaviours in Northern Ireland: 14–15 Year Old School Children*. Craigavon: Love for Life.

Maxwell, C. (2006) Understanding Young Women's Sexual Relationship Experiences: The Nature and Role of Vulnerability. *Journal of Youth Studies*, 9: 2, 141–58.

Maxwell, C. and Aggleton, P. (2009) *Young Women and Their Relationships: Power and Pleasure. Key Issues For Practitioners and Policy Makers*. London: Thomas Coram Research Unit.

McAlister, S., Gray, A.M. and Neil, G. (2007) *Still Waiting: The Stories Behind The Statistics of Young Women Growing up in Northern Ireland*. Belfast: Youth Action Northern Ireland.

McNamee, H. (2006) *Out on Your Own: An Examination of The Mental Health of Young Same-Sex Attracted Men*. Belfast: The Rainbow Project.

NICCY (Northern Ireland Commissioner for Children and Young People) (2009) *Children's Rights: Rhetoric or Reality. A Review of Children's Rights in Northern Ireland 2007/08*. Belfast: NICCY.

NIO (Northern Ireland Office) (2008) *Explanatory Guidance to the Sexual Offences (Northern Ireland) Order 2008*. Belfast: NIO. Accessed Sept. 2013 at: www.nidirect.gov.uk/explanatory_guidance_to_the_sexual_offences_ni_order_2008.pdf

NIO and DHSSPS (2008) *Tackling Sexual Violence and Abuse. A Regional Strategy 2008–2013*. Belfast: DHSSPS.

NISRA (Northern Ireland Statistics and Research Agency) (2008) *Young Persons' Behaviour and Attitudes Survey Bulletin: October–November 2007*. Belfast: NISRA.

NISRA (2010) *Young Persons' Behaviour and Attitudes Survey Bulletin October-November 2010*. Belfast: NISRA.

North and West Belfast Health Action Zone (2007) *How is it For You? A Survey Into The Sexual Health Service Needs of Young People in North and West Belfast*. Belfast: North and West Health Action Zone.

North and West Belfast Health Action Zone (2008) *RSE: Making it a Reality. Relationships and Sexuality Education in North and West Belfast*. Belfast: North and West Health Action Zone.

Office of the Children's Commissioner (2012) *I Thought I Was The Only One, The Only One in The World*. London: Office of the Children's Commissioner.

Palmer, T. (2001) *No Son of Mine! Children Abused Through Prostitution*. Barkingside: Barnardo's.

Pearce, J. (2009) *Young People and Sexual Exploitation: 'It's Not Hidden, You Just Aren't Looking'*. London: Routledge.

Ringrose, J. et al. (2012) *A Qualitative Study of Children, Young People and 'Sexting'*. London: NSPCC.

SBNI (Safe Guarding Board for Northern Ireland) (2013) *SBNI Strategic Plan 2013–2016*. Belfast: SBNI.

Schubotz, D. (2012) *Messed up? Sexual Lifestyles of 16-Year Olds in Northern Ireland*. ARK Research Update 80, Belfast: ARK. Accessed Sept. 2013 at: www.ark.ac.uk/publications/updates/update80.pdf

Schubotz, D., Rolston, B. and Simpson, A. (2004) Sexual Behaviour of Young People in Northern Ireland: First Sexual Experience. *Critical Public Health*, 14: 2, 177–90.

Schubotz, D., Simpson, A. and Rolston, B. (2002) *Towards Better Sexual Health. A Survey of Sexual Attitudes and Lifestyles of Young People in Northern Ireland*. London: FPA.

CHAPTER 7

Generation X Y Z – To be or Not to be a Volunteer?

Christine Irvine and Wendy Osborne

Generation labelling is not new and is used to demonstrate where each generation may have different attitudes and behaviours. A joint report from the Chartered Institute of Personnel and Development (CIPD) and Penna Recruitment Communications suggests that there are four key generational groups currently in the workforce – Veterans, Baby Boomers, Generation X, and Generation Y (2008: 6). Since then, a Generation Z has also been identified, to differentiate those born around the mid 1990s from Generation Y, who were born around the early 1980s. Of course, there is variation between commentators on which years define the generations so these dates have to be taken as a general indication only.

The 2009 Young Life and Times (YLT) survey recorded the attitudes of 16 year olds who would form part of the last cohort of Generation Y. One of the defining characteristics of this group is their understanding and competence in information technology (IT). In particular, the internet, mobile phones and social networking define both how they communicate and how they access information. However the difficulty about any form of labelling is that it cannot be definitive: for example, human nature, personality, family background, socio-economic environment, personal circumstances and experience all contribute to defining who each of us is and how we behave. So, young people in Northern Ireland have views and will make choices about key issues, which include volunteering, that may follow certain generational trends such as the use of the internet and social networks. Nevertheless, there are other factors that are very important as to why they may or may not choose to volunteer.

The 2009 YLT survey included a module of questions on volunteering, and this has been the only year that a module in YLT or any other survey of 16 year olds in Northern Ireland has been devoted to this topic. Therefore, the survey results present an important snapshot of the attitudes and experiences of volunteering by 16 year olds in the region. This chapter has been structured around some of the key findings from this module. In addition, other regional, national and international research on youth volunteering more broadly (of those aged 16 to 25 years) will be used to discuss some key issues and trends. The chapter concludes with an outline of some key points with respect to the future development of youth volunteering.

Introduction

2012 and 2013 were significant years for volunteering. The publicity for volunteering during the London Olympic Games helped to rebalance the discussion around volunteering, representing a much more positive public image of it. In 2012, 390 people from Northern Ireland became Olympic and Paralympic Games Makers. The World Police and Fire Games (WPFG) held in Belfast in 2013, and Derry/Londonderry becoming the first UK City of Culture in 2013 offered a wide range of volunteering opportunities and helped to raise the profile of volunteering, so much so that 5,200 people completed applications to volunteer for the WPFG, half of them had never volunteered before.

So what is volunteering? One useful definition is that it is . . .

The commitment of time and energy, for the benefit of society and the community, the environment, or individuals outside (or in addition to) one's immediate family. It is unpaid and undertaken freely and by choice.

(DSD, 2012)

There are two different types of volunteering, (a) *formal* (carried out with, or under the auspices of an organisation/group) and (b) *informal* (carried out outside an organisation, often at neighbourhood level (ibid).

The last major public survey in Northern Ireland which looked at 'formal' and 'informal' volunteering separately was carried out in 2007 and found that 23 per cent of 16 to 24 year olds volunteered formally. This was up by seven percentage points from 1995, and made this age group the second most likely to volunteer after 35 to 49 year olds (24%) and several percentage points above the average volunteering rate for the whole population (21%) (Volunteer Development Agency, 2007). This mirrors the global picture in 2011, where the age group of 35 to 49 year olds is consistently the most likely to volunteer, followed by 15 to 24 year olds (CAF, 2012). Among respondents to the 2009 YLT survey, 30 per cent reported that they formally volunteered, with rates of informal volunteering much lower at 17 per cent. Generally in Northern Ireland, informal volunteering rates tend to be higher than for formal volunteering (Irvine and Schubotz, 2010). Due to different methodological approaches, accurate comparisons of survey results cannot be made in relation to rates of volunteering. Other recent research on volunteering has been conducted through the 2011 Census of Population for Northern Ireland, and the Department for Social Development (2012). However, results were not publicly available for the 16 to 25 age group at the time of writing. Nevertheless, local surveys consistently report that many thousands of young people volunteer in Northern Ireland.

Policy relevance

The first volunteering strategy for Northern Ireland *Join in, Get Involved, Build a Better Future* was launched in March 2012 (DSD, 2012). This provided a structured policy framework for the development of volunteering up to 2016. The Strategy includes a specific objective (2.1a) to enable children and young people to become involved in volunteering and help them to develop skills and gain experience through their voluntary activity. Key performance indicators associated with this objective include an increase in the number of young people volunteering and in the number participating in the Millennium Volunteers (MV) Programme (DSD, 2012). The MV initiative began in 1999, and is funded by the Department of Education as a Northern Ireland-wide programme designed to promote and recognise sustained volunteering among young people of all backgrounds aged 14 to 25 years. At the time of writing, 353 organisations offering volunteering opportunities for young people were MV delivery partners. However, among YLT respondents in 2009, only 13 per cent had heard of it.

Over recent years there has been a substantial public policy interest in youth work including the consultation document relating to the review of youth work, *Priorities for Youth* (DENI, 2012) which sets out key reforms in the delivery of youth service provision in Northern Ireland. The wider work through the Children and Young People's Strategic Partnership aims to better co-ordinate services to improve the outcomes for children, young people and their families. These outcomes comprise:

- Health.
- Enjoying, learning and achieving.
- Living in safety and with stability.
- Experiencing economic and environmental wellbeing.
- Contributing positively to community and society.
- Living in a society which respects their rights.

(CYPSP, 2012)

There has been recognition of the role of the voluntary and community sector in supporting these priority areas. According to *A Charter for the Voluntary Youth Sector*, nine out of every ten workers in the youth sector are volunteers (YouthNet, 2011). Volunteering can and should be a win win situation for young people, organisations and the wider community. In the longer term, many children and young people who benefit as participants of youth programmes move on to volunteer, often within the same groups that they themselves benefited from.

The Big Society was the flagship policy idea of the 2010 United Kingdom (UK) Conservative Party general election manifesto and became part of the legislative programme of the Conservative-Liberal Democrat Coalition Agreement. The stated aim was to create a climate that empowers local people and communities, building a 'big society' that will take power away from politicians and give it to people. While some have responded to the policy favourably, its aims have been queried and disputed by other commentators. Although many of the initiatives and programmes coming from this policy are relevant to England only, the *National Citizen Service Programme* is one example which included Northern Ireland. The Programme was piloted for the first time in Northern Ireland in 2012, and is a voluntary eight-week summer programme run in England (16 to 17 year olds) and Northern Ireland (15 to 16 year olds). 250 young people from Northern Ireland took part. The project was funded by the Cabinet Office and supported by the Department for Social Development. The programme includes a range of elements, including an opportunity for young people to design and deliver two volunteer projects to benefit their community.

Citizenship and civic engagement

Local and central governments have made efforts to engage young people in civic fora and youth councils as a way of getting their views heard by elected representatives and to engage them on current affairs and public policy. As voting rights in Northern Ireland do not start until the age of 18 years of age, other forms of civic participation and activism are important to encouraging young people to develop a civic identity from the earliest opportunity (O'Brien, 2011). It is important for young people to have a say on issues that affect them (see Chapter 2 of this book) not least because this also helps to build their connections with others in their communities as early as possible. Some of the key benefits that come from volunteering are associated with building networks, friendships and connections – the building blocks of social capital.

Northern Ireland-based research has found that the propensity to volunteer is linked to some degree with the propensity to be more active as a citizen. Across a range of forms of civic participation, including attending public consultation events, being involved in raising an issue with MPs, MLAs, signing a petition, attending a lawful demonstration, and engaging in a form of public consultation, volunteers were more likely to get involved than non-volunteers.

Case Study 1

Fixers (www.fixers.org.uk) is a movement of young people aged 16 to 25 who are tackling issues they feel strongly about with the aim of making a difference for others. Many have been through difficult times, and have used that experience to campaign on issues that matter to them, like being homeless, domestic abuse, or drink and drug misuse. As part of their campaigns, and working with professional producers, they are creating some fantastic films, songs, music videos and other resources. Several have won awards. Thanks to a recent grant from the Big Lottery Fund, *Fixers* is expanding over the next three years throughout the UK – including Northern Ireland.

Vicki is 24 years old. Her campaign is called *Sign'ary School*. She was taught British Sign Language (BSL) at an early age. It has allowed her to converse with people who have hearing difficulties in personal, social and professional situations. She wants to create a resource that helps teachers deliver lessons in BSL to Key Stage 2 pupils at primary schools:

'Young people should be able to develop at least a basic competence in sign language in order to be able to communicate with anyone they encounter with a hearing impairment. Working with Fixers, I want my resource to target primary school teachers and parents in particular. But obviously, I want to reach out to the wider public as well.'

In her review of youth volunteering in 2004, Katharine Gaskin, an author of much volunteering research within the UK, stated that:

Commentators have emphasised that the process of political and civic engagement is not instant but develops as young people mature. Most importantly it begins when young people have opportunities to develop 'a strong sense of identity, self worth, responsibility and confidence. Few would disagree that volunteering in all its incarnations can provide these opportunities but only if policy makers and organisations see young people as a valuable resource and are prepared to make the changes necessary to welcome their involvement.

(Gaskin, 2004: viii)

Gaskin goes on to suggest that the culture of volunteering, either amongst family or friends, makes individuals more predisposed to volunteer themselves, and argues that it is possible that a culture of being an active citizen is also something that is inherited. The importance of having role models within family, friendship or wider networking circles that can champion volunteering cannot be under-estimated. Neither can the need for strong leadership by Government which values and supports volunteering and volunteer involving organisations. This necessitates a government that values volunteers and that seeks to involve the 'community' in new and dynamic ways of being an active citizen, whilst also benefiting those that wish to help.

Societal attitudes

Unfortunately, the positive aspects of youth are often overshadowed by the negative, especially as the most powerful mass media tool – the news media – tends to focus on the latter. These negative messages influence the perception that adults have of young people. Research conducted by Machin and Malmersjo (2006) found that volunteer-involving organisations are generally more proactive in approaching the media than the UK media are at approaching them.

Research conducted by YouGov in 2008 with over 2,000 UK adults showed that the public holds a negative view of children, despite the vast majority of children making positive contributions to their communities, attending school, taking part in activities and volunteering. The findings showed that just under one half (49%) of people agree that 'children are increasingly a danger to each other and adults'; 43 per cent agree that 'something has to be done to protect us from children'; more than a third (35%) of people agree that 'nowadays it feels like the streets are infested with children'; 45 per cent agree that 'people refer to children as feral because they behave this way'; and nearly half of people (49%) disagree with the statement that 'children who get into trouble are often misunderstood and in need of professional help' (Barnardo's, 2008). Perhaps it is not surprising, therefore, that three quarters of respondents to the 2010 Young Life and Times survey thought that the media portrays young people mostly negatively (see Chapter 5 for a more detailed discussion of this).

Case Study 2

Shakeel is 14 years old. He started volunteering with *Save the Children* as part of his *Duke of Edinburgh Award* which he is completing through school.

'*It was a great feeling of taking part in something positive and I loved the opportunity to learn new skills and meet new people. The 12-week experience led me on to wanting to volunteer more and so, that's why I signed up for the Millennium Volunteers programme.*'

Shakeel said he had enjoyed meeting new people of all ages and backgrounds. The experience gave him a taster of what it would be like to do a job in the future.

'*I gained things from volunteering such as learning organisational skills and time management, which are very important in the working world today.*'

Young volunteers appear to be invisible to the rest of the world for several reasons. Firstly, there is a general cultural norm that perceives a 'volunteer' as being anyone aged 16 years of age or over. Secondly, we also see this norm reflected in the lack of volunteering opportunities that are marketed to young people who are below 16 years old. It is in part understandable that organisations are put off by fear of additional risk and insurance implications for involving under 16 year olds. These organisations may also struggle with matching ability and skill with organisational needs. Thus, families, institutions such as schools, and the volunteering infrastructure all have a part to play in facilitating and enabling younger children to engage with volunteering. Thirdly, rates of volunteering for people aged under 16 years are not known, as public surveys generally only collect information on those aged 16 years of age or over. As a result, little is known about the volunteer activities, motivations, or barriers of those who are under 16 years old. However, younger children can benefit from volunteering in the same way older children do. Research carried out with 8 to 12 year olds in Canada reported a range of benefits from volunteering, the most commonly reported being fun and enjoyment of the rewards. The most significant barriers related to perceptions others had on what younger children could do as volunteers (Shannon, 2009).

Thus, the inclusion of questions within the 2009 YLT survey provides a timely and important record of the behaviour, motivations and attitudes of 16 year olds in relation to volunteering.

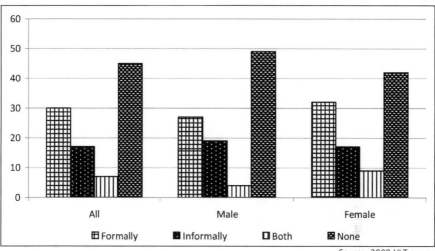

Source: 2009 YLT survey

Figure 7.1   Rates of volunteering (%)

Young people and volunteering – who does it?

Among the YLT respondents in 2009, just over one half (54%) had volunteered in the past 12 months; 30 per cent had done so formally through an organisation, 17 per cent had volunteered informally in their community and seven per cent had volunteered both formally and informally. Mirroring general volunteering patterns, females were more likely to say that they volunteered (58%) than males (50%) – see Figure 7.1.

The survey data also allow us to look at socio-demographic factors associated with levels of volunteering. Previous population-based research found that people from higher socio-economic groupings tend to report higher levels of volunteering than those from other backgrounds (Volunteer Development Agency, 2007). Matching this, one strong pattern within the YLT data is that of a 'class divide' in terms of the rates of youth volunteering. Figure 7.2 shows that young people from poorer backgrounds were more likely to report that they were not involved in any type of volunteering (60%) compared to young people from more well-off backgrounds (35%). In addition, grammar school students were over twice as likely as secondary schools students to say that they formally volunteered in the past year (40% and 19% respectively) (Irvine and Schubotz, 2010). However, at the time of writing, the Millennium Volunteers programme involved 34 grammar schools; 46 secondary schools

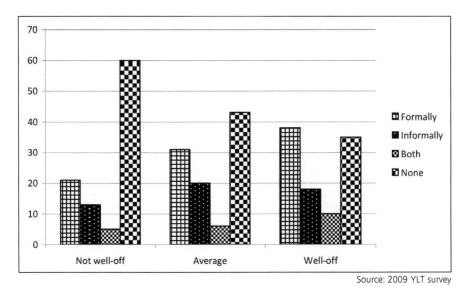

Source: 2009 YLT survey

Figure 7.2 Volunteering rates and types, by family-financial background (%)

and eight special schools. The comparatively high number of secondary schools involved in the programme may help to reverse this trend.

Where people lived also influenced whether they volunteered and the type of volunteering they were involved in. There were higher levels of formal volunteering in the outskirts or suburbs of towns compared to inner city areas or rural areas. The barriers to volunteering for young people that live in more rural areas and inner cities are persistent, different to those of other sub-groups, and therefore need to be addressed differently. This is a historic issue which is caused by wider socio-economic factors that cannot be addressed by the volunteering infrastructure alone. For example, rural communities suffer from a lack of accessible public transport making it harder to access formal volunteering opportunities. Lack of access to bus services is more acute in rural areas than in urban areas, but it is a much more serious problem in Northern Ireland than in Great Britain: 42 per cent of rural respondents in Northern Ireland said there were no bus services which could take them to local shops and services, compared to just 16 per cent of rural respondents in Great Britain (Northern Ireland Assembly Research and Library Service, 2010). It could be argued that the lower volunteering rates in inner cities are an artefact of the lower economic status of young people and their families living there.

Table 7.1   What benefits do you get from volunteering*?

	%
Meeting people/making friends	70
Really enjoying it	69
Broadens experience of life	67
Sense of personal achievement	67
Improves confidence	64
Chance to learn new skills	62
A recognised qualification/improving employment prospects	54
Other	4

*Respondents could identify more than one benefit
Source: 2009 YLT survey

Benefits of volunteering

Those volunteers who took part in the YLT survey identified a wide range of benefits coming from volunteering, as shown in Table 7.1. The most common benefits were meeting people and making friends (70%), enjoyment and fun – 'really enjoying it' – (69%), broadening one's experience of life (67%) and having a sense of personal achievement (67%). This pattern matches that shown in other surveys conducted with young people (Hill, Russell and Brewis, 2009).

One young person commented that 'it helps me give my views and opinions which are listened to and appreciated'.

Just over one half (54%) of the young volunteers taking part in the YLT survey specifically saw getting a recognised qualification or improving their employability as a benefit of volunteering, and this fits into wider discussions about education. One key objective of the educational system is the preparation of young people for employment, by developing skills and by supporting them to maximise their potential (Stewart, 2008). The school curriculum in Northern Ireland has a specific remit in developing the 'Local and Global Citizenship' of pupils and promoting opportunities for personal development. Both are seen as being critical to the broader preparation for 'Learning for Life and Work' (ibid).

For nearly two thirds of respondents (62%), the chance to learn new skills was important, reflecting the concern caused by the world economic recession. Northern Ireland, as elsewhere, has experienced considerable youth unemployment. At the time of writing, youth unemployment among 18 to 24 year olds was 20.3 per cent (DETINI, 2013) and has led to commentators talking about a 'lost generation' (Barysch, 2012). Accurate and up-to-date figures on the number of young people aged 16 to 19 years old, who are not in education, employment or training (NEET) are harder to access due to the lack of an aggregated Government database. However, the 2012 *Pathways to Success Strategy*, which is the specific Government action plan for reducing NEET rates, estimated that rates were 14.3 per cent as of December 2012 and had been increasing year on year since 2000 (DEL, 2012).

Evidence consistently shows that young people who are thinking about employment and careers are interested in volunteering as a way of enhancing their CVs and university application forms, and are using this experience to set themselves apart in competition for work or study. A survey with 141 14 to 24 years olds who attended the 2011 Millennium Volunteers celebration event further demonstrated the perceived or actual benefits of volunteering with respect to the development of employability skills. In that survey, 97 per cent reported that volunteering had increased or would increase their ability to get paid work and 95 per cent stated that volunteering had increased or would increase their ability to get a place on a university or college course (Volunteer Now, 2011).

There is now an established evidence base for the role of volunteering as a preventative and interventionist measure to some of the issues which children and young people face and which can affect their education and future employment prospects. The majority of the programmes run in the Youth Sector in Northern Ireland rely on volunteers (YouthNet, 2011). In particular, young people 'at risk' benefit from the work of voluntary youth workers. It is young people who are from the poorest backgrounds who are most likely to make up the group of young people not in education, training or employment. This is also the group that is least likely to volunteer, and therefore do not benefit from the learning and experiences that come from it (Horgan, Gray and Conlon, 2010). A large-scale evaluation of the Scout Association found many benefits gained by disadvantaged groups from participating in the Scouts organisation. For example, Scouting had helped to divert some young people from crime and had enhanced their life chances in terms of employment and education. Furthermore, a common view was that these young people were given opportunities for personal development, community engagement and access to activities that would not have been provided to the same degree through other fora (PACEC, 2011).

The following quote from a young Scout Network leader highlights the benefits of volunteering from their perspective:

I get a sense of achievement [from scouting], and this has helped with my CV and has helped when I have applied for certain jobs. At a couple of interviews I was asked about my involvement in Scouting and they were impressed, well they seemed to be! I do think that it helped me in the end to get the job I'm in now.

(PACEC, 2011)

Case Study 3

Cait is 20 years old. She has been volunteering since she was 15 years old. The majority of her volunteering involves working with children and adults with either physical and or mental disabilities. She is also a committee member with a cancer charity. Cait thinks that her mother and grandmother were 'the most inspirational influences', regarding her desire to volunteer.

'Volunteering by far surpasses any other opportunities. You can volunteer and gain experience in any career that you are interested in. You make new friends, acquire excellent contacts, who will always be there for you, as you settle into full time work. Volunteering in any field is so rewarding. I work and I am a full time student; being able to take time away from study and pressures is wonderful. I get the opportunity to use all the skills and new knowledge I have gained in theory and apply it, seeing first hand the results. For me, volunteering has renewed my personal belief in myself, in my abilities and has strengthened my understanding and passion to teach children with Special Needs.'

When unemployment is looking more and more pervasive, it could be argued that volunteering as a form of active citizenship has never been more important for developing young people's sense of identity and citizenship (Lister et al., 2002). In their three-year longitudinal study with young people aged 16, 19 and 22 years in Leicester, they found that self-identification as a citizen varied in relation to factors such as whether or not they had achieved waged employment and paid tax, voted or had an effective say, but also included whether they had undertaken voluntary work.

Many young people are looking for more challenging and interesting opportunities which involve decision-making and leadership roles. This is a general trend being observed across the volunteering sector which requires organisations to consider new ways of involving volunteers which can utilise a greater range of skills and aptitudes.

Motivations to volunteer

Like the benefits highlighted above, the motivations for volunteering reported through the YLT survey are equally varied and include a mix of altruism and self-interest. A more nuanced picture emerges when the YLT research is analysed by gender and family financial background. The results suggest that motivations for youth volunteering are influenced by these two factors. Table 7.2 shows that respondents from well-off backgrounds were predominantly driven to volunteer by career motivation (81%) whereas respondents from not well-off backgrounds mainly volunteered for altruistic reasons (78%), namely in order to help other people and to improve things. This difference is less pronounced when male and female motivations to volunteer are compared; however, females are still more CV and career-motivated in their volunteering

Table 7.2 Motivation for Volunteering. By gender and family-financial background*

	%				
	Gender		Family-financial background		
	Male	Female	Not-well-off	Average	Well-off
I wanted to improve things and help people	59	68	78	63	62
I wanted to meet people and make friends	39	44	37	40	48
The cause was really important to me	19	25	33	18	28
My friends/family also volunteer	32	34	34	31	36
I thought it would give me a chance to learn new skills and use existing ones	55	62	70	56	61
I was asked to help	49	40	37	43	45
It helps me to get on in my career and build up my CV	67	77	65	72	81
It's part of my religious belief or philosophy of life to help people	24	23	15	20	31
Other	10	11	11	8	15

*Respondents could identify more than one motivation.
Source: 2009 YLT survey

than males (77% and 67% respectively). Interestingly, the only motivation to volunteer more common for males than females was 'being asked to help'.

For several respondents, volunteering was a necessary part of a separate activity, such as *Duke of Edinburgh* or *Pope John Paul II* awards. However, for another respondent, volunteering was about giving back to an organisation that they had previously been involved in: 'I went to Scouts for 10 years, so wanted to volunteer to give back again.' For another young person, their motivation was that 'it makes me happy when I can see people smile.'

Building community relations

Inter-community relations in Northern Ireland remains an issue for both the government and society as a whole, whether between Catholics and Protestants, or between local communities and those from other countries who have settled in Northern Ireland (McGrellis, 2011). (For a fuller discussion on community relations, see Chapter 1.) The 'ageing' nature of our population means that both the youngest and oldest members of our society are becoming an increasing proportion of it. Therefore, intergenerational relations are also an important area to develop. The external evaluation of the Beth Johnston Foundation's Linking Generations Northern Ireland Programme demonstrates how volunteering programmes can be a useful conduit for developing respect and understanding between age groups (Juniper Consulting, 2011).

Results from the 2009 YLT survey suggest that volunteering programmes have the potential to make a significant contribution to community cohesion and therefore to more favourable attitudes towards a shared future in Northern Ireland. Over one half (57%) of young people who had volunteered in the previous 12 months reported that they had seen an increase in their network of friends and 42 per cent stated that they had more contact with people from a different community or religious background. Irvine and Schubotz (2010) found that, compared with non-volunteers, YLT respondents who were volunteers were more likely to report more regular contact with young people from a different background. One in five respondents who had never volunteered said they 'very often' socialised with people from a different background compared to 39 per cent of young people that volunteered either formally or informally. They also found that the young people from poorer backgrounds, although less likely to formally volunteer, tended to benefit more in terms of getting the opportunity to meet other young people from different religious backgrounds (ibid).

Table 7.3 Contact with people from a different community background, by family-financial background

	%		
	Not well off	Average	Well-off
Increased	53	41	39
Remained the same	42	52	58
Decreased	0	1	0
Don't know	5	6	33

Source: 2009 YLT survey

The changing face of volunteering

Technology is accounting for a greater proportion of how young people spend their leisure time and how young people choose to communicate and access information. Although social networking is growing across all age groups, younger people are more likely to access social networking sites, with 61 per cent of 15 to 34 year olds claiming to do so, compared to 40 per cent of all adults. 16 to 24 year olds are the most likely age group to say that technology is changing the way they communicate (72% agreement) (OFCOM, 2012). This is borne out by the fact that teenagers and young adults are leading the changes that are being seen in communication habits. They are increasingly socialising with friends and family online and through text messages, despite also saying that they prefer to talk face to face (ibid). Use of technology by young people is happening at an increasingly young age: a survey with young people aged 11 to 16 years in Northern Ireland found that the majority use social media networks, with Facebook being the most popular (91%) (CSU, 2011). Thus, the use of information technology, and social media in particular, present an opportunity for organisations to communicate with young people in relation to volunteering.

Methods of communication about volunteering

All YLT respondents were asked how they would like to receive information on volunteering, and all current volunteers were also asked how they had found out about the opportunity to volunteer. As Table 7.4 shows, an interesting pattern emerged regarding the difference between the actual and the preferred sources of information about volunteering, which is relevant when

Table 7.4 Main and preferred sources of information about volunteering

	%	
	Actual source of information*	Preferred source of information**
School	62	69
Internet	11	43
Articles/Adverts in the media	8	42
From a friend or family member	48	n/a***
Someone else already involved in volunteering	42	n/a***
Word-of-mouth	n/a	41
Through a church or religious organisation	33	n/a

*calculated as a percentage of those who volunteer
**calculated as a percentage of all respondents
***n/a: not an option for this question
Source: YLT 2010

one thinks more broadly about communication with young people and volunteering marketing strategies. The results show that school has an important role in encouraging and enabling young people to volunteer and it is also one that young people would choose (62% reported this as an actual source for volunteering and 69 per cent reported it as a preferred source). Interestingly, although the internet and articles/adverts in the media were popular sources to find out about volunteering in theory (43% and 42% respectively), in practice they accounted for just a small percentage of how young people had actually heard about volunteering (11% and 8% respectively).

Qualitative research conducted with young people has highlighted the need for clear and nuanced recruitment messages when communicating with them which take differences into consideration, such as gender and the financial background of the family. The benefit of involving peer recruiters as a way of targeting new people to volunteer has also been raised as an area for development (Volunteer Now, 2010). This type of initiative may help to capitalise on the power of word of mouth communication which remains one of the most commonly reported sources for finding out about volunteering.

Models of volunteering

The growth of technology has implications for how volunteering opportunities are marketed. The technological age is also driving new innovation in the models of volunteering that are being offered, although as yet, this is not common practice. There has been no research carried out in Northern Ireland on the prevalence of technology-based volunteering, and the regional database of volunteering opportunities currently contains few online or remote opportunities compared to non-remote options. Nevertheless, online volunteering through mobile telephones and the Internet offers the opportunity to engage and enable more people, including young people, to volunteer. The remote and micro-sized nature of those types of opportunities may offer the flexibility needed to overcome barriers such as location and time availability (Jochum and Paylor, 2013). Any form of remote volunteering could offer a more accessible way for young people in rural areas to volunteer who may otherwise miss out due to physical barriers like lack of transport. It is also an alternative option for young people with a disability who may find it difficult to get from place to place. Nevertheless, these new models do not negate the need for society and volunteer-involving organisations specifically to react to wider equality issues such as making adaptations to buildings and roles to help people with disabilities to volunteer.

There is an alternative school of thought which questions the impact of remote volunteering on the development of the volunteer compared to other more traditional ways of volunteering which require people to meet, or for people to go to a physical place to volunteer. There are also question marks over the potential of such activities to truly benefit a cause or to support charitable work in an impactful way (ibid). One-off or group volunteering opportunities are often suitable for people of all ages, as they can be tailored to different age groups, require flexible commitment and tend to be projects that are short-term in nature. There is also increasing interest from families, particularly parents with children, who wish to find meaningful, educational, purposeful activities to do as a family. Volunteering can provide a conduit for this aim. An evaluation of the National Trust Family Volunteering Pilot Programme found that direct marketing to families was key and was particularly effective when promoted through schools and community events (Bird, 2011).

It remains to be seen how young people's lifestyles, motivations, interests and engagement in social media will shape and influence volunteering for them in the future. For the moment, there is clearly a need for as much variety in how young people can get involved as is possible, which requires introducing volunteering at the earliest opportunity and involves the co-ordinated effort of society, families, educational institutions and the volunteering infrastructure. As Gaskin put it:

> A civic service programme should be part of an overall youth volunteering 'meta strategy' which enables young people to have a volunteering career which begins in school and offers opportunities at every juncture as they progress through their teens and into adulthood. This would encompass full time, part time and occasional volunteering, team based and individual, local, national and international volunteering and e-volunteering.

(Gaskin, 2004: vii)

Young people and volunteering – why not?

Importantly, the YLT survey also explored reasons why young people were not involved in volunteering. This information can help organisations tailor their activities to be more attractive to young people.

Although not always fully understood, young people can be as 'time-poor' as adults. The 2008 YLT survey found that 80 per cent of young people said that school work and exams made them stressed.

Table 7.5 shows that 'not having enough time' was the main reason given by YLT respondents for not volunteering. This matches the findings within a more recent report on sports volunteering which found that some young people, particularly those participating in sports, as well as having educational and employment demands, are more able to do short bursts of volunteering

Table 7.5   What factors help explain why you do not volunteer?

	%
I have too many other commitments e.g. work, at school, at home	54
I've never thought about it	36
Wouldn't know how to find out about it	30
None of my friends are volunteering	13
Haven't got the right skills or experience	11
I'm already doing enough	10
I think I'm too young	5
It's not a cool thing to do	2
Other	4

Source: 2009 YLT survey

rather than committing to sustained volunteering over time (Houlihan and Bradbury, 2013). A lack of time has also been reported as the most common barrier to volunteering for people aged 16 and over (DSD, 2007).

Although time constraints are the most common barrier to volunteering for young people (53%); the YLT survey also found that there is a pool of 16 year olds who reported to have never thought about volunteering (36%) or stated that they wouldn't know how to find out about volunteering opportunities (30%). From a practice point of view, these responses suggest that current marketing and communication of volunteering is not getting through to some sections of youth. One respondent cited a particular financial issue:

> *I am not wasting my time doing something for free; I have to pay adult prices for everything but can't do adult things, so I need more money.*

Conclusion

So what can we learn from research on youth volunteering about Generation Y in Northern Ireland and their support for, and relationship with, volunteering? What are the factors that interplay to determine if and in what way young people get involved in volunteering?

Local research tells us that young people in Northern Ireland are interested in volunteering. The majority see the benefits in terms of personal development and employability and they are interested in doing different activities that provide both variety and flexibility. The internet, mobile phones and social media are their means of communication and these are the vehicles they use to access information. Exposure to volunteering either through personal experience, networks and role models (family, friends, school or organisations they are involved with) does motivate young people to say 'yes' to being a volunteer.

Volunteering can be a beneficial life choice for young people, and in turn, their involvement in these activities has positive benefits for the community; not least in building a sense of belonging and responsibility, as well as creating role models for the next generation!

To maximise this mutuality of benefit, policy makers, institutions and organisations working with young people and those organisations that involve volunteers need to take cognisance of some issues. Providing information about the benefits of, and accessibility to, volunteer opportunities has to be a priority, as are new ways of linking young people through school, careers guidance. Families remain an untapped resource with respect to volunteering, and so there is a lot of scope for organisations to consider promoting volunteering directly to families. There is also a need to offer young people the widest range of volunteer opportunities which includes giving them the opportunity to input into organisational decisions and take leadership roles where they can be challenged and feel they are trusted and have control (Waters and Bortee, 2010). At the same time, it is important to gather evidence on the full benefits of volunteering for young people as we need to target and improve the levels and diversity of young people involved, particularly from more deprived backgrounds or those within the NEET category.

Finally, the skills and development needs of people who manage volunteers must remain high on the policy, practice and research agendas to deliver the volunteering experience that meets the expectations of young people (Brewis, Hill and Stevens, 2010). All of these steps would also make a valuable contribution to the successful implementation of the Northern Ireland Volunteering Strategy and Action Plan (2012–16) by getting more young people involved as active citizens.

References

Barnardo's (2008) *The Shame of Britain's Intolerance of Children.* YouGov Poll, Release Date 17 Nov 2008. Accessed Sept. 2013 at: www.barnardos.org.uk/news_and_events/media_centre/press_releases.htm?ref=42088

Barysch, K. (2012) *Youth Unemployment: Europe's 'Lost Generation'?* Public Service Europe. Accessed Sept. 2013 at: www.publicserviceeurope.com/article/2804/youth-unemployment-europes-lost-generation

Bird, C. (2011) *Family Volunteering Pilot: Getting Families More Actively Involved in the National Trust's Work.* Swindon: The National Trust.

Brewis, G., Hill, M. and Stevens, D. (2010) *Valuing Volunteer Management Skills.* London: Institute for Volunteering Research.

CAF (Charities Aid Foundation) (2012) *World Giving Index: A Global View of Giving Trends.* Kent: CAF.

CIPD (Chartered Institute for Personal Development) and Penna (2008) *Gen Up: How The Four Generations Work. Joint Survey Report.* London: CIPD.

CSU (Central Survey Unit) (2011) *Young Person's Behaviour and Attitudes Survey. Bulletin October–November 2010,* Belfast: NISRA. Accessed Sept. 2013 at: www.csu.nisra.gov.uk/YPBAS%202010%20Headline%20bulletin.pdf

CYPSP (Children and Young Person's Strategic Partnership) (2012) *Northern Ireland Children and Young People's Plan 2011–2014.* Belfast: CYPSP. Accessed Sept. 2013 at: www.cypsp.org/publications/cypsp/action-plan/cypsp_action_plan_2011-201 4.pdf

DEL (Department for Employment and Learning) (2012) *Pathways to Success: Preventing Exclusion and Promoting Participation of Young People.* Belfast: DEL. Accessed Sept. 2013 at: www.delni.gov.uk/del-pathways-to-success-v6.pdf

DETINI (Department for Enterprise, Trade and Investment) (2013) *Labour Force Survey – April–June. 2013*. Belfast: DETINI. Accessed Sept. 2013 at: www.detini.gov.uk/deti-stats-index/stats-labour-market/stats-labour-mar ket-unemployment.htm

DSD (Department for Social Development) (2007) Findings from the workshop with Community Development and Health Network. Accessed Sept. 2013 at: www.dsdni.gov.uk/???-workshop-???-health-network.doc

DSD (2012) *Join In, Get Involved, Build a Better Future*, Belfast: DSD. Accessed Sept. 2013 at: www.dsdni.gov.uk/join-in-get-involved-2012.pdf

DENI (Department of Education for Northern Ireland) (2012) *Priorities for Youth. Improving Young People's Lives Through Youth Work*. Bangor: DENI. Accessed Sept. 2013 at: www.deni.gov.uk/pfy_consultation_document_english_pdf

Gaskin, K. (2004) *Youth Volunteering, Volunteering and Civic Service: A Review of the Literature*. London: Institute for Volunteering Research.

Hill, M., Russell, J. and Brewis, G. (2009) *Young People, Volunteering and Youth Projects: A Rapid Review of Recent Evidence*. London: Institute for Volunteering Research.

Horgan, G., Gray, A. and Conlon, C. (2010) *Young People not in Education, Employment or Training: Policy Brief*, Belfast: ARK. Accessed Sept. 2013 at: www.ark.ac.uk/pdfs/policybriefs/policybrief3.pdf

Houlihan, B. and Bradbury, S. (2013) *10 Years of Teamwork: McDonald's National Grassroots Football Partnership 2002–201*. Loughborough: Loughborough University.

Irvine, C. and Schubotz, D. (2010) *Youth Volunteering: Making a Difference to Community Relations*. ARK Research Update 69, Belfast: ARK. Accessed Sept. 2013 at: www.ark.ac.uk/publications/updates/update69.pdf

Jochum, V. and Paylor, J. (2013) *New Ways of Giving Time: Opportunities and Challenges in Micro-Volunteering: A Literature Review*. London: Institute of Volunteering Research and NCVO.

Juniper Consulting (2011) *Evaluation of the Linking Generations Northern Ireland Programme. Final Evaluation Report*, Accessed Sept. 2013 at: www.centreforip.org.uk/res/documents/publication/LGNI%20Evaluation%20Re port.pdf

Lister, R. et al. (2002) *Negotiating Transitions to Citizenship. Report of Findings*. Accessed 08.02.2013 at: http://archive.excellencegateway.org.uk/media/post16/files/NegotiatingT ransi-tions_to_Citizenship.pdf

Machin, J. and Malmersjo, G. (2006) *Promoting Volunteering: Experiences of Liaising With The Media on Volunteering Issues*. London: Institute for Volunteering Research for the Voluntary Action Media Unit.

McGrellis, S. (2011) *Growing Up in Northern Ireland*. York: Joseph Rowntree Foundation.

Northern Ireland Assembly Research and Information Service (2010) *Rural Development Issues and Challenges in Northern Ireland*. Briefing Paper 125/10, Belfast: Northern Ireland Assembly Research and Information Service.

O'Brien, K. (2011) *Engaging North Carolina's Generation Z in Civic Life*. NC State University Institute for Emerging Issues. Accessed 11.09.2013 at: http://iei.ncsu.edu/wp-content/uploads/2013/01/EngagingNCGenZ.pdf

OFCOM (2012) *Communications Market Report 2012*. Accessed Sept. 2013 at: http://stake-holders.ofcom.org.uk/binaries/research/cmr/cmr12/CMR_UK_2012.pdf

PACEC (2011) *The Scout Association: Impact Assessment Evaluation of The Scouts Association – Final Report*. London: The Scout Association.

Shannon, C. (2009) An Untapped Resource: Understanding Volunteers Aged 8 to 12. *Nonprofit and Voluntary Sector Quarterly*, 38: 5, 828–45.

Stewart, (2008) *Report on the Millennium Volunteers and the School Curriculum in Northern Ireland*. CELT Association Broadening Horizons.

Volunteer Development Agency (2007) *It's All About Time*. Belfast: Volunteer Development Agency. Accessed Sept. 2013 at: www.volunteernow.co.uk/fs/doc/publications/itsallabout-timefullreport200 7.pdf

Volunteer Now (2010) *Notes From Workshop at Launch of 'Youth Volunteering – Making a Difference to Community Relations*. Unpublished paper.

Volunteer Now (2011) *Millennium Volunteers Celebration Event Survey*. Unpublished paper.

Waters, R.D. and Bortee, D.S. (2010) Building a Better Workplace for Teen Volunteers Through Inclusive Behaviour. *Nonprofit Management and Leadership,* 20: 3, 337–55.

YouthNet (2011) *A Charter for the Voluntary Youth Sector*, Belfast: YouthNet. Accessed Sept. 2013 at: www.youthnetni.org.uk/Site/29/Documents/youthnet%20charter%20sept%2011.pdf

CHAPTER 8

A 16 Year Old's Perspective of Living in Northern Ireland

Ewan Nixon

Perceptions and pressures

Teenagers have a variety of issues to worry about; from their school work, their appearance, relationships, the influences of friends, the media, parents and the constant worry of being unable to fit into the categories of 'child' and 'adult'. One issue is the risk of being unfairly judged by those around you. Somehow society has pictured us as lazy, ungrateful slobs whose only goals in life are to eat, sleep and spend hours on end staring at the computer screen. The media is constantly shoving the idea of the 'perfect teenager' in our faces – and not only that – glorifying celebrities who we should all supposedly aspire to be like. Unfortunately, it is inevitable that some of us will buy into this propaganda, and perhaps this is what gives us our reputation. However, I will try and put across the very true point that most teenagers are not who they are depicted to be in the adult world.

Adolescence is, metaphorically speaking, a no man's land between childhood and adulthood. According to your parents and society, you are too young to enjoy the freedoms of your elders. Yet at the same time, you are old enough to do chores; have a part time job – and all of that at the same time; concentrate on the never ending flow of exams, essays, and coursework that constitute GCSEs and A levels; all the while knowing that once they're finished, you'll have to work until you're 65 or older.

Growing up in Northern Ireland

While being a teenager is already difficult to begin with, the circumstances and religious/political pressures provided by life in Northern Ireland only make this awkward phase of life even more difficult. An issue that is specific to Northern Ireland within the United Kingdom context is its emphasis on religion. In many parts of Northern Ireland, a neighbourhood and the cultural groups within it can be segregated into different areas. Teenagers can feel the effect of this in that their friends will usually only be of a certain religion (for example, either Catholic or Protestant). Their peers can put pressure on them to commit acts of violence or vandalism, and these incidents are typically what create hard-hitting headlines. However, the majority of us would just prefer that the violence would stop. From my own personal experience, my friends and peers (whatever religion they may be), have all shared the opinion on this matter that the conflicts of Northern Irish society have grown tiresome and unnecessary.

Friends

Teenagers, including myself, are largely dependent on the comfort of having friends who they can relate to and talk with as the stress of feeling so alienated from society would be too much to cope with by ourselves. This brings us back to the fact that this is a phase of life where you are neither considered a child nor an adult, and that parents are able to pick and choose what activities we can and can't do. This proves very frustrating due to the illogical aspects of these ideals. The support that we receive from having close friendships can be vital to our emotional well-being, and this is very useful when attempting to find someone who can relate to our thoughts and issues. Perhaps this is why it is often preferable to confide in a friend rather than an adult who would be less likely to understand the issue on the same level as a fellow teenager.

Fitting in

Another problem that teenagers face is the pressures of both their social status and their ability in school. If we do not conform to 'trends' and the many aspects of teenage life that the media has blown out of proportion, it is possible to become a social outcast in the eyes of your school mates. This pressure also runs in parallel with the focus on academic studies that is enforced/encouraged by parents and teachers, and many of us struggle to find a way of balancing out the social and educational aspects of our lives. The pressure of trying to fit in is a priority for teens and one that cannot be ignored – and as parents may observe, few of us will put ourselves in danger of losing our social status over problems in teenage life such as bullying, conflict at home/school and the search for independence. Parents and other adults seem to have difficulty in understanding these pressures and this can be particularly frustrating to teenagers as the feeling of alienation is only emphasised by this. This misunderstanding is possibly what has caused many young people to act out as a method of asking for attention. This has caused an unfortunate reputation for teenagers, which, in turn, only helps to aggravate the friction between us and adults.

Adult-teenager relationships

It is understandable, however, that the problems faced by teenagers grow more difficult for adults to understand, as time goes on and nostalgia begins to take hold of their memories. Conversely it is also easy to see that from a teenager's perspective, adults have many issues that are not experienced by most adolescents, such as household bills, housekeeping, and the difficulties of parenthood. In my opinion it would be helpful if some adults learned to be more empathetic towards us, because without this, feelings of mistrust can develop as many adults don't see teens' issues as 'real' problems. It would be helpful if more adults could try and relate to teenagers by looking back to remind themselves that they were once in a similar situation. However, inspirational behaviour from adults comes in many forms – there are a variety of people that we can look up to, mentors that shape our outlook on life and help formulate our plans. From influential leaders to family members – all can help teenagers relate to adults through helping them to see how their lives and problems run in parallel, whatever their age.

As well as the split between education and social life, teens also experience a split between family life and friends as well – values and morals can change in these situations, and how a teenager behaves with their friends is rarely reflective of their personality at home. This is possibly why it is such a shock to parents when teenagers are influenced by peers into disorderly behaviour, and it is another way in which mistrust between teens and parents can develop. Specifically, in Northern Ireland, teenagers can very easily be affected by the conflicts of the country – many of their peers can have some sort of view on the politics of the situation which can again put pressure on teens to want to fit into certain groups while still maintaining their family lifestyles.

Prejudice

Teenagers in Northern Ireland (depending on their ethnicity and cultural background) can also face prejudice from those around them; again, this brings the issues of bullying and alienation back into focus. Immigrants, particularly teenagers, are very vulnerable to abuse from their peers, due to the historically high rate of prejudice amongst the younger population of Northern Ireland. However, integrated education and more open-minded opinions have become much more widely accepted in the last three decades, and it is a positive sign that teenagers in Northern Ireland are starting to learn the values of equality and break free from past conflicts that have plagued the country for so long.

Because of this, I believe that adults should be encouraged to value the fact that teenagers are the future of our country and that our enlightened attitudes will carry on into future generations with us. Therefore investing in our youth in a way that promotes healthy relationships with others who are different can only prove to be a building block that will improve life for everyone. It is only too easy to fall into the trap of thinking that 'the best is yet to come' while waiting for adulthood to arrive.

Dealing with family relationship breakdowns

Teenagers in Northern Ireland, and the rest of the world for that matter, also face family and relationship problems, sometimes on a daily basis. Issues such as divorce have a massive impact on teenagers, sometimes even resulting in mental health issues due to the overwhelming nature of the pressures on a young person's life. Relationship problems can become even more stressful alongside exams, social lives and the general sense of alienation that most teenagers feel from the adult world. One in three marriages now end in divorce and that means we all know someone who has been affected by family issues. It is even more important that friendships will sustain throughout these times of difficulty for the teenager who is inadvertently caught up in the cross-fire. Friends, who will give support or even just provide a sense of normality during times of upheaval and great change, will sustain the teen in these times of difficulty. Of course, other unfortunate and sad circumstances can and do happen, and the beneficial comfort that the teenager's circle of friends provides is an invaluable grounding influence that cannot be replaced.

All in all, while the problems in Northern Ireland have still not been completely repaired, adults need to see that the teenagers here have a lot of responsibility. They are creating a more peaceful and equal Ireland as well as dealing with all of the other issues that teenagers around the world must face on the road to adulthood.

Conclusion

Dirk Schubotz

Using an annual study of 16-year olds to monitor and inform social change in Northern Ireland

The Young Life and Times (YLT) survey is now the longest running annual cross-sectional attitude survey among 16 year olds in the UK and Ireland. For more than a decade YLT has covered a broad variety of subject areas, and the previous chapters in this book provided a snapshot of this diversity. Due to the limitation in space in this volume, we could only invite a small number of authors to make contributions. We chose topics that we felt are also of relevance outside the immediate geographical context in which the data were collected. Children's and young people's rights; mental health; volunteering; and sexual exploitation of young people have all been subjects that have in recent months or years appeared in the media again and again. Some of these topics were connected to mass events, for example the 2012 Olympic and Paralympic Games in London where many young volunteers were celebrated as the '*games makers*'. Others, such as the issue of sexual exploitation has appeared and reappeared in the media due to significant and large-scale criminal investigations, such as the institutional sex abuse cases, which have highlighted the vulnerability of young people and society's failure to protect them.

Apart from these well-covered subjects, our book also offers insights into less well researched subject areas, such as loneliness among young people and young people's right and need to play – a topic that is often wrongly thought only to be relevant to smaller children. However, no book based on data collected in Northern Ireland would be complete without an update on young people's views on community relations and the Northern Ireland Peace Process. Fifteen years after the Good Friday/Belfast Agreement, this review of evidence is very timely.

The Appendix to this book provides the bare technical details of the YLT survey. However, in this concluding chapter I reflect on the day-to-day challenges of running a social attitude survey among 16 year olds over the ten-year period from 2003–2012. I discuss the ambitions of the YLT project and describe some concrete examples of how YLT has been used to monitor societal change and inform policy making in Northern Ireland.

The beginning: giving young people the opportunity to express their views

As noted in **Chapter 2**, the United Nation's Convention on the Rights of the Child (UNCRC) provides a clear legal framework for the participation of children and young people in decision making on matters that affect them. However, although the Convention has been ratified by the vast majority of countries in the world, too often the opinions of children and young people are still not considered when decisions are being made about them. With this in mind, in 1998, academics from the two universities in Northern Ireland – the University of Ulster and Queen's University Belfast – conducted the inaugural YLT survey. The survey was initially targeted at 12–17 year olds living in households of adults who took part in the Northern Ireland Life and Times (NILT) survey, a large-scale annual attitude survey run in Northern Ireland also since 1998.

In line with the ambition to give young people a chance to voice their opinions on matters that affect them, the inaugural YLT survey was mainly concerned with issues related to children's and young people's rights and their participation in school. However, other questions focused on perceptions of community relations in Northern Ireland. After all, in 1998 the year of the first YLT survey, the Northern Ireland population had just voted in favour of the Belfast Agreement (also known as 'Good Friday Agreement' and was taking first steps towards the institutionalisation of the Peace Process. As **Chapter 3** in this volume shows, the Northern Ireland Conflict had had particularly adverse effects on young people. Crucially, in 1998 the first ever YLT respondents were also asked whether they felt it would be useful to have a regular survey like this of young people's views, to which more than three quarters (76%) responded that they felt it would be. With this convincing vote, the annual YLT survey was born.

In its original format the YLT survey ran for just three years. The age gap between the youngest (12 years) and oldest (17 years) participants became problematic and meant that universally relevant and appropriate questions were difficult to formulate. Twelve year olds who had just started post-primary education dealt with completely different issues from 17 year olds who either had already left school and were working, training for a job, or were preparing for a university or further education career. Furthermore, ethical issues arose from the mode of the survey. As young people completed the survey at home in the presence of their parents some questions could not be asked or were unlikely to be answered frankly by the YLT respondents. Hence, a methodological review took place in which policy makers from Government departments as well as representatives from charities working on behalf of children and young people took part. As a result, the YLT survey was re-established in 2003 as an independent postal survey of 16 year olds. The age of 16 was chosen for a number of reasons. In the UK, at age 16 young people reach the age of consent and gain a number of rights. They can therefore make important decisions themselves, although, as in most other countries, they have to wait until they are 18 years of age to gain basic political rights such as the right to vote. At age 16 young people also go through an important status passage where they reach the end of compulsory post-primary schooling and can decide to leave school to find a job or take on an apprenticeship or else continue with post-primary education in order to gain access to tertiary education at university or a college of further and higher education.

Ambitions and methodological challenges

In 2000, the academics from the University of Ulster and Queen's University formalised their co-operation and formed a network called ARK. ARK's mission is *to make social and political information on Northern Ireland available to the widest possible audience*. This is done through a variety of activities, which include the hugely popular and internationally acclaimed CAIN resource (Conflict Archive on the Internet – www.ark.ac.uk/cain) as well as three annual social attitude surveys, one of which is *Young Life and Times*. All data as well as results tables and topical lay-friendly publications based on the modules in the YLT survey, are freely made available on ARK's website – without any access barriers such as registrations, logins etc. The easy availability of the information, as well as the rigour with which the projects have been undertaken for over a decade, have helped to establish ARK as one of the most used social policy resources in the UK, although its reach goes well beyond this. Monthly page downloads for the YLT survey alone currently average 15,000, whilst CAIN – ARK's most popular resource – far exceeds this with approximately 48,000 unique visitors each month and 17 million visitors in total since CAIN started. Arguably, in many ways, ARK set best practice standards with regard to the availability of information before the sharing of data and information became as commonplace as it is now.

With regard to the YLT survey, the ambitions of the ARK team are to:

• Run the study as an academically sound project.
• Cover areas that are relevant to young people.

- Be informative to social policy makers, but also critical towards existing social policy.

The fieldwork for most surveys among young people is conducted through schools. ARK, however, decided against this and successfully applied for permission to draw a random sample from Child Benefit recipients for its annual YLT survey. Until 2012, Child Benefit was a non-means-tested benefit for people bringing up children in the UK and was paid for each child. A survey sample based on the Child Benefit Register has significant advantages over school-based samples. Firstly, it is more inclusive, since school absentees and young people outside mainstream schooling are not excluded. Secondly, as the surveys are sent out directly to the 16 year olds, legally, there are no further gatekeepers (such as school principals) that may prevent young people from completing the questionnaire, if they so wish. Thirdly, since the surveys are likely to be completed individually in the respondent's home, classroom interactions, which may lead to group bias and influence the way 16 year olds respond to sensitive questions, are much less likely to occur.

However, despite these advantages, the YLT sampling strategy poses challenges. One of the difficulties with using administrative data such as the Child Benefit Register for research purposes is having to rely each year on civil servants' co-operation to create the address file of respondents. Data security breaches which occurred at Her Majesty's Revenue and Customs (HMRC) meant that data security regulations were changed and updated several times in the previous ten years. The YLT project was affected by this, and subsequent delays in the fieldwork were inevitable. In the end, HMRC and other government agencies involved in the administration of Child Benefit data have always provided the necessary dataset. But not having the guarantee that this will happen in the future, not knowing exactly what support documentation would be requested each year and whether or not data safety at Queen's University and the University of Ulster will be deemed appropriate, has at times been stressful.

Communication with respondents and their parents

As discussed above, the age of 16 years was chosen for several reasons. One of the main reasons was that young people reach the age of consent when they are 16 and can make decisions by themselves on whether or not they wish to take part in a survey like this. Our experience has been that in most cases, 16 year olds that we invite to take part in the YLT study **do** open their own

mail and respond independently, if they choose to do so. However post to 16
year olds is sometimes being opened by parents and monitored. Parents may
opt out of the survey on behalf of their children or may get in touch to acquire
more details. This is more likely to happen when the respective survey
questionnaire includes questions on what parents see as sensitive subject areas.
In the past decade, parents were most likely to get in touch when subject areas
such as self-harm, sexual health, sex education or substance use were included
in the survey questionnaire. In one case, a Freedom of Information request was
lodged with the Queen's University about the study and its ethical approval.
Over the years, both young people and their parents have become more
outspoken and more inquisitive about the study, in particular about why ARK
has access to the Child Benefit Register for sampling purposes. This is perhaps
a result of the very public security breaches which have led to the disappear-
ance of computer discs and laptop computers which held sensitive personal
administrative data. This has added to the generally increased awareness of
data security among both young people and adults.

However, questions about the legitimacy of the survey are not the most
common reasons why respondents and their parents get in touch with the
survey team. Every year parents of young people with learning disabilities also
get in touch to opt out of the survey on behalf of their adolescent sons or
daughters altogether or to request to what extent they can support them in
the completion of the survey, if they wish to take part. Often these young
people attend special schools which are frequently excluded from school-based
surveys. Whilst not all young people with disabilities are able to fill in the
survey, the advantage of the YLT sample is that they are not excluded per se
and therefore have a greater likelihood of being included.

Another common reason why parents may get in touch is due to
inaccuracies of the details held about them and their children on the Child
Benefit Register. Whilst it is parents' responsibility to keep the information on
the Register up-to-date, of course not all recipients of Child Benefit do this.
Parents may get divorced or re-marry and change their own and their children's
names in that process, but they may not amend the details held on the Child
Benefit Register. Parents may adopt or foster children and, again, change the
children's names in that process, but then fail to update their Child Benefit
record. The consequence of this is that letters with incorrect names are being
sent out, which may lead to awkward situations. Over the years we had a
number of cases where, through the communication in relation to the YLT
survey, 16 year olds have found out that they were adopted or that a parent

who they believed to be their biological parent, was in fact not. On one occasion, a letter was sent out to a young person who had in fact died a few weeks beforehand. For whatever reason, these cases lead to difficult situations and unpleasant communications: reminding parents during these conversations that it is their responsibility to update Child Benefit Records can be difficult.

Communication with young people does not end with the completion of the survey. From the first survey onwards we have seen it as good practice to offer young person-friendly feedback on key results. Respondents can of course access the website as everybody else but, in addition, we have produced young-person friendly summary fliers which are posted out to everyone who requests this. In addition young people are invited to seminars on their request.

Funding and survey topics

Funding a research project like YLT regularly over a ten-year period poses obvious challenges. In line with our ambition to provide an opportunity for young people to express views on matters that are relevant to their lives, but equally to provide a resource that informs policy making, the range of funding sources has been very broad and has included government departments and quangos as well as charitable organisations and large funders of academic research, both in the EU and the UK. The YLT funding strategy can therefore be described as three-dimensional consisting of:

- Proactive large scale funding applications such as applications to EU funding bodies and UK Research Councils.
- Tender responses, sometimes jointly with other organisations.
- An open-door policy for suitable requests from charities, university re-searchers, government departments and government quangos (e.g. The Northern Ireland Commissioner for Children and Young People (NICCY), the Electoral Commission and the Patient and Client Council (PCC)) that want to use the YLT survey as a vehicle to explore new subject areas or to monitor young people's attitudes to and experiences of specific issues.

The greatest difficulty with regard to running YLT over the previous decade has continuously been to attract core-funding for the survey infrastructure. Smaller charities in particular have occasionally been unable to meet all survey module costs, and without flexibility and creativity with regard to funding models the survey would not have endured through difficult financial times.

The diversity of funders is also reflective of the variety of topics that have been covered over the years. As discussed above, when the YLT survey was first initiated around the time when the *Belfast Agreement* was signed, an obvious focus was on community relations. Fifteen years after the Agreement, relations between Catholics and Protestants remain as topical as ever, and the YLT survey has become an important tool for Government to monitor changes in attitudes to, and perceptions of, community relations over time. Indicators from the YLT survey help to monitor the effectiveness of government programmes and initiatives, such as the *Shared Future* Policy and its successor programme (OFMDFM, 2005, 2010), the Department of Education's *Community Relations Equality and Diversity Education* (DENI, 2011) and NICCY's ambitions to raise awareness about the UNCRC among children and young people. A new dimension to community relations in Northern Ireland are the relations with people from minority ethnic backgrounds, as over the previous decade an increasing number of people have migrated to Northern Ireland, both as a result of the Peace Process and the EU enlargements.

However from early surveys onwards, YLT respondents commented that community relations alone hardly reflected what the '*Life and Times*' of 16 year olds in Northern Ireland are about. Young people requested the inclusion of topics such as alcohol and drug consumption, peer pressure, sex education, self-harm and suicide, sexual orientation, hobbies and whether young people planned to stay in Northern Ireland in future, to name but a few. Gradually over the years, the YLT surveys have covered such topics that are relevant to young people including mental health (including self-harm), attitudes to play and leisure, sexual health and sexual exploitation, volunteering, attitudes to politics, informal caring, and child poverty. On a regular basis we also revisited the questions on rights and participation.

Throughout the recent decade, it has been important to ARK to ensure that young people's thoughts on what should be included in future YLT surveys were also considered and taken seriously. Whilst large scale surveys are not the most participatory research instruments, by including questions suggested by young people in each survey and by proactively seeking funding for research in areas that 16 year olds said were important to them, we feel that we have managed to inform policy making in Northern Ireland to some extent, and we have raised issues on behalf of 16 year olds.

Challenges may arise when funders are not happy with the results of the research they commission or with the interpretation of the data. Furthermore, whilst funding from large independent funders, such as the Economic and Social Research Council (ESRC), a European Funding programme or the Nuffield Foundation is generally unproblematic in that respect, being funded by just one local funder, for example a Northern Ireland government department, may potentially compromise the independence of a project – even if there is no reason to be suspicious about the integrity and the rigour of the work undertaken. The perception that the study has become 'government survey' or a survey of a pressure group or charity which subsequently follows a particular rationale could be damaging. However, ARK has been very careful to avoid such situations and the mix of funding sources, if anything, has contributed to ARK's and the YLT survey's reputation of being a good and reliable source to inform policy making.

Examples for policy information and debate

In the last section of this essay, I will describe some examples in more detail which show how the YLT survey has been used for policy information and debate. Over the previous decade, the range of projects we conducted was wide-ranging and included the following:

- Work with *Save the Children* on their campaign to end child poverty.
- Work with *PlayBoard* on play and leisure (see Chapter 5 in this book).
- Work with *Barnardo's* on sexual risks and exploitation (see Chapter 6 in this book).
- Work on behalf of the Department of Education on Community Relations, Equality and Diversity Education (CRED).
- Work on behalf of the Electoral Commission on young people's attitudes to politics and elections.
- Joint work with the National Children's Bureau (NCB) on behalf of the Northern Ireland government (OFMDFM) on attitudes to minority ethnic groups.
- Work with the *Volunteer Service Bureau* on volunteering among young people (see Chapter 7 in this book).
- Work on behalf of the Northern Ireland Commissioner for Children and Young People (NICCY) on shared education policy initiatives.

Some of these projects were undertaken as mixed methods projects, for example the *Attitudes to Difference* study undertaken jointly with the NCB on attitudes to minority ethnic groups (NCB NI and ARK YLT, 2010). This project – as some others before and after – involved young people directly as peer researchers. Qualitative methods were employed in addition to the YLT survey to explore issues in more depth. We have discussed our participatory approach in more detail elsewhere (Schubotz, 2011; Schubotz and Devine, 2008).

However, the four examples for policy information I concentrate on at the end of the present chapter focus on community relations, school bullying, mental health and the sexual exploitation of young people.

Example 1: Monitoring community relations over time

As a society coming out of significant and violent conflict, Northern Ireland has increasingly been seen as a model for a peaceful transformation. Although progress in the Peace Process has often been temporary and a case of 'two steps forward and one step back', young people have been seen as the carriers of the new societal structures. Many people, including some young people themselves, often talk about young people as being 'the future'. Whilst we insist that young people have very much the right (and desire) to be involved in the building of a new and shared Northern Ireland in the 'here and now' and not just 'in the future', it is certainly true that the expectation to practice more sharing rests on the younger generations. It is therefore crucial to monitor their attitudes towards community relations and sharing. A range of core questions about community relations have been asked in every YLT survey. This allows us to track changes in attitudes over time. Government has been using the YLT responses as indicators for their community relations and good relations policies, as already stated above. As described in Chapter 1, data from YLT shows that, overall, the proportion of 16 year olds who feel that community relations are better now than they were five years ago has increased slightly over time. Fluctuations can be attributed to significant political events, such as the collapse of the devolved government or violent protests around the time when the field work was undertaken. However, an interesting finding has been that – with the exception of one year – 16 year olds actually have more negative perceptions of community relations than their adult counterparts. This is despite – or maybe because of – the fact that the vast majority of YLT respondents will not have consciously or directly experienced the worst effects of the Northern Ireland conflict, simply because they are too young.

Whilst it would have been unrealistic to expect that all the effects of the Northern Ireland conflict, which lasted for several decades, would be eradicated within one generation, for the Northern Ireland government these results suggest that more peace-building work needs to be undertaken with young people. Recent examples are the *Community Relations, Equality and Diversity (CRED) Education* programme (DENI, 2011) as well as initiatives for increased *shared education* between fundamentally segregated schools and school sectors. Question batteries on both of these latter initiatives have been included in very recent YLT surveys on behalf of the Department of Education and NICCY, so ARK is again trusted with monitoring the effects of these projects on attitudes and experiences of young people.

Example 2: School bullying

A project titled *'Being Part and Parcel of the School'* was jointly undertaken with the UK's National Children's Bureau (NCB) on behalf of NICCY. The project arose out of a consultation undertaken by NICCY among school children in Northern Ireland which revealed that school bullying had been an important issue. Despite all efforts to tackle bullying in schools, the prevalence rates have hardly changed, so an increased active involvement of pupils in policy making on school bullying and in anti-bullying practices and awareness raising in schools was seen as a way to tackle this serious problem. Our research project followed a participatory approach, so in addition to the YLT survey, qualitative research was undertaken jointly with peer researchers in schools. As a result of this research project, NICCY developed a poster campaign and a guidance resource on the involvement of pupils in schools in general, and on school bullying in particular, which was disseminated to all schools in Northern Ireland and is still being used (Sinclair, 2008).

Example 3: Mental health

The third project focused on the mental health of young people. ARK was commissioned to undertake this work on behalf of the Patient and Client Council (PCC). The PCC is a publicly funded, but independent organisation that was set up to monitor progress in the provision of mental health and disability services in Northern Ireland. The so-called *Bamford Review* (2006) had given evidence for serious gaps in service provision in Child and Adolescent Mental Health Services, and the high rates of self-injury and suicide among young people in Northern Ireland had caused particular concern. The PCC was set up with the specific task to promote the involvement of patients, clients, carers and the public in the design, planning, commissioning and delivery of health and social care services, and YLT was seen as an appropriate vehicle to collect young people's experiences and views in this regard. A report was published by the PCC (Schubotz, 2010) and widely disseminated. In 2008, the YLT survey also first asked questions on self-harm in Northern Ireland and therefore closed a research gap and provided comparable data to other parts of the UK and the Republic of Ireland where these questions had been asked before (see Chapter 3 in this book).

Example 4: Sexual exploitation of young people

The final example relates to very recent study of sexual exploitation which has been discussed here in detail in Chapter 6 by its author Helen Beckett. YLT was approached by Barnardo's with regard to their study on sexual grooming and the sexual exploitation of vulnerable young people. The purpose of the YLT involvement was to get an understanding of grooming and sexual exploitation among the general population of young people, something which had not been done before in Northern Ireland. Again, school-based surveys would have been unable to provide this data due to the reluctance of many schools to engage with sexual matters, as the experience of Northern Ireland's Young Persons Behaviour and Attitude survey (YPBS) shows. On the back of this research, we successfully applied for funding to the ESRC to run a teacher training day as well as undertake a Knowledge Transfer project with Brook Northern Ireland in which we developed an education resource on sexual risks together with young people.

Conclusion

This chapter provides just a brief snapshot of the experiences of running a social attitude survey among young people for over a decade in Northern Ireland, a society coming out of conflict. Surveys are often regarded as anonymous and therefore unsuitable vehicles to engage with children and young people. However, the example of the YLT survey shows how a cross-sectional annual attitude survey can be a useful instrument to influence policy making. Over the years we have taken young people's views very seriously – not just in decisions about the design and the content of the annual surveys, but also in the dissemination of findings, which includes feedback directly given to respondents. The direct involvement of young people as peer researchers in mixed methods projects connected to YLT has further strengthened the project's reputation and outreach. This has helped to establish the survey as an instrument that the government has increasingly relied on and felt confident in using to monitor their policies on children and young people. Perhaps all this would have been impossible to achieve without a reliable and committed staff team that remained basically unchanged for the past ten years. Despite this, finding funding for each new survey remains as complex and challenging in year 11 as it was in year one.

References

Bamford Review of Mental Health and Learning (2006) *Child and Adolescent Mental Health Services: A Model Service.* Belfast: DHSSPS.

DENI (Department of Education for Northern Ireland) (2011) *Community Relations, Equality and Diversity in Education.* Bangor: Department of Education for Northern Ireland. Accessed Sept. 2013 at: www.deni.gov.uk/cred_policy_doc1.pdf

NCB NI and ARK YLT (2010) *Attitudes to Difference. Young People's Attitudes to and Experiences of Contact With People From Different Minority Ethnic and Migrant Communities in Northern Ireland.* London: National Children's Bureau.

OFMDFM (Office of the First Minister and Deputy First Minister) (2005) *A Shared Future: Improving Relations in Northern Ireland.* Belfast: OFMDFM.

OFMDFM (2010) *Programme for Cohesion, Sharing and Integration.* Consultation Document, Belfast: OFMDFM.

Schubotz, D. (2010) *The Mental and Emotional Health of 16-Year Olds in Northern Ireland. Evidence from the Young Life and Times Survey.* Belfast: Patient and Client Council.

Schubotz, D. (2011) Involving Young People as Peer Researchers in Research on Community Relations in Northern Ireland. In Heath, S. and Walker, C. (Eds.) *Innovations in Youth Research.* Houndmills: Palgrave Macmillan.

Schubotz, D. and Devine, P. (2008) Giving Young People a Voice Via Social Research Projects: Methodological Challenges. In Schubotz, D. and Devine, P. (Eds.) *Young People in Post-Conflict Northern Ireland. The Past Cannot Be Changed, But The Future Can Be Developed.* Lyme Regis: Russell House Publishing.

Sinclair, R. (2008) Tackling Bullying in Schools: The Role of Pupil Participation. In Schubotz, D. and Devine, P. (Eds.) *Young People in Post-Conflict Northern Ireland. The Past Cannot Be Changed, But The Future Can Be Developed.* Lyme Regis: Russell House Publishing.

Appendix

What is the Young Life and Times (YLT) survey?

This Appendix provides technical information about the Young Life and Times (YLT) survey, including the sampling frame and response rates. In particular, the changing administrative and legal context of using this sampling frame are outlined.

All too often the opinions of young people are ignored when decisions are made about many of the issues involving them. Thus, the aim of the annual YLT survey is to record the views of 16 year olds in Northern Ireland. Undertaken in the current format since 2003, the initial focus of YLT was on community relations issues such as politics, sectarianism and education. However, the range of topics has expanded over the years in order to reflect contemporary debates. In particular, by inviting respondents to make suggestions for the following year's survey, we make sure that the topics covered are relevant to the lives of 16 year olds in Northern Ireland today.

Links with other surveys

The YLT survey is one of three annual attitude surveys undertaken by ARK (www.ark.ac.uk).

The *Northern Ireland Life and Times* (NILT) survey records the attitudes and values of adults aged 18 years and over in Northern Ireland. This is an annual survey and began in 1998. The range of topics included in NILT varies each year, although many question modules are repeated over time in order to monitor changing attitudes on specific social policy issues. In particular, questions on community relations and political attitudes are included each year in order to track attitude change on these issues taking place within the rapidly shifting social and political environment of Northern Ireland. Full details on the NILT survey can be found on the website at www.ark.ac.uk/nilt

The *Kids' Life and Times* (KLT) survey gives younger children a voice, and an opportunity to help influence policies that affect them. This is an annual survey of all Primary 7 children (who are aged 10 or 11 years) in Northern Ireland covering what they think about school as well as other pertinent issues. The survey began in 2008, and as with YLT, we invite respondents to suggest topics for the next year's survey. In this way, we can ensure that the questions relate to children's lives. KLT is an online survey carried out in schools. In addition, children schooled at home are also invited to participate. For more information about KLT, and to view the results, see www.ark.ac.uk/klt

Technical details

Sample

The sampling frame for the YLT survey is the Child Benefit Register. Child Benefit is a benefit for people bringing up children and is paid for each child. Therefore, the Register contains information on all children for whom Child Benefit is claimed. Until January 2013, this was a universal benefit, meaning that it was not means-tested, and a parent/guardian was eligible to apply for every child.*

---

* Since 7 January 2013, a High Income Benefit Charge is liable where at least one parent (or their partner) has an annual income of more than £50,000. Where the annual income is more than £60,000, this charge amounts to 100 per cent of the Child Benefit payment.

In 2003, this Register was the responsibility of the Social Security Agency (SSA) of the Department for Social Development (DSD). However, in 2004, while DSD still maintained the database, the responsibility for the payment of Child Benefit transferred to the Inland Revenue. Thus, it was necessary to negotiate access to this Register from Inland Revenue, which involved an explanatory memorandum being prepared relating to the Tax Credits (Provision of Information) (Evaluation and Statistical Studies) (Northern Ireland) Regulations 2004. Inland Revenue was merged with Her Majesty's Customs and Excise in 2005 to form Her Majesty's Revenue and Customs (HMRC).

In autumn 2007, two computer discs containing personal details of tens of thousands of Child Benefit recipients were lost by the United Kingdom (UK) government. Following this incident, regulations relating to sensitive and personal data were tightened. As a result of these revised data security procedures, ARK had to re-apply to access the Child Benefit dataset for further YLT surveys. This application was considered by respective units within HMRC and by the legal team of DSD. Following the granting of permission by HMRC, DSD applied for a sweep of the Child Benefit data on behalf of the YLT survey team.

The sample for the 2011 and 2012 surveys were provided to ARK directly by HMRC, as part of a Service Level Agreement between ARK and HMRC. Within this agreement ARK laid out details for the safety and security of the personal data of respondents. This included arrangements for the safe transport and storage of the files, as well as destruction of the address file after completion of the data collection.

From 2003 to 2007, all young people who celebrated their 16th birthday in February of each survey year were invited to take part. In 2008, this criterion was extended to include all young people who had their 16th birth in March of the survey year, in order to increase the number of completed surveys.

From 2003 to 2008, fieldwork was carried out from August to October each year. In 2009, operational delays in acquiring the sample meant that fieldwork ran from October to December, and this fieldwork period has been retained since then.

Survey and advance letter distribution

From 2003–2010, survey information sheets containing a passive opt-out clause were sent to all eligible YLT respondents alongside their survey questionnaire and response envelope. However, from the 2011 survey onwards, advance opt-out letters were sent out prior to the actual survey questionnaire being distributed. Each respondent is assigned a unique identifier, and this is marked on the advance letter and on the paper questionnaire. The advance letters explain why and how the addressee was selected to take part in the YLT survey; what topics are covered in the survey; and what the aim of the YLT project is. Incentives to take part in the survey are also detailed. Whilst a very small proportion of respondents actively opt out at that stage, the opt-out letters have the benefit that some address inaccuracies can be identified and corrected. Most common opt-out reasons, if any is given, are that the respondent is either too busy or just not interested in taking part. Some respondents' parents or carers get in touch to opt out on behalf of children with learning or sensory disabilities or to ask whether assisting their child in the completion of the survey was permitted.

Approximately three weeks after the initial communication, all respondents who have not opted out of the survey receive the paper questionnaire alongside a FREEPOST return envelope and a letter from the YLT project team, detailing again the aims of the project, the three possible methods of completing the questionnaire, as well as details of the prize draw (five cash prizes of

£100 each year plus any other incentives that may be available in the respective survey year, depending on the available funding). For example, in order to encourage online completion, an incentive scheme began in 2009 whereby the first 100 online respondents received a £10 shopping voucher (if the respondent was happy to provide their contact details).

Again, approximately three weeks after the initial questionnaire, those who have not responded by that stage receive a reminder letter as well as another paper questionnaire and FREEPOST return envelope. In the past we experimented with a final reminder postcard, but not only did this not significantly increase response rate, it also resulted in an increasing number of complaints from young people and their parents, so that this practice was stopped.

Completing the questionnaire

Respondents are able to choose one of three methods for completing the questionnaire:

1. They can take part by phone, having quoted their unique identifer.
2. They can complete the questionnaire online – quoting their personal identifer to access the questionnaire on the YLT website.
3. They can complete the paper questionnaire that was sent to them in the initial pack and post it back in the FREEPOST envelope.

Multiple responses from respondents (for example, one online and one postal response) are prevented by daily recording of the receipt of completed questionnaires. Once a respondent has submitted an online questionnaire, their unique identifier is automatically disabled.

Survey content

Each year the survey focuses on four or five topics. The range of topics varies every year, although attitudes towards community relations are always covered – see Table A1. Background demographic information is also collected each year.

At the end of each questionnaire, respondents are given the opportunity to identify questions they feel are suitable for inclusion in the following year's survey. Many of these have been incorporated into future surveys, for example, self-harm, and sexual risks.

Response rate

From 2003 to 2007, approximately 2,000 questionnaires were sent out, and around 4,000 since 2008, reflecting the changed selection criterion.

Table A2 shows that the most popular mode of completing the survey was using the paper questionnaire, followed by completing the survey online. Very few respondents completed the survey on the phone. The response rates have been fluctuating over the years, perhaps reflecting various interests in the survey content, different efforts to boost response rates and a general trend towards lower response rates for this type of survey. However, overall, the YLT surveys have yielded very good to respectable response rates for a postal survey of this type. Furthermore, the continuous analysis of the collected background data suggests that drops and increases in response rates have not affected any particular respondent groups, but have occurred across all groups.

Table A.1 Survey content (2003–12 YLT survey)

	Year of survey									
	2003	2004	2005	2006	2007	2008	2009	2010	2011	2012
Background	✓	✓	✓	✓	✓	✓	✓	✓	✓	✓
Community relations	✓	✓	✓	✓	✓	✓	✓	✓	✓	✓
Cross community contact	✓	✓	✓	✓	✓	✓	✓	✓	✓	
Education	✓	✓	✓	✓	✓	✓	✓	✓	✓	
Environment and global issues			✓							
Family		✓	✓	✓	✓	✓	✓	✓	✓	
Health (including mental health)		✓	✓	✓	✓	✓				
Identity	✓				✓					
Leisure and play			✓		✓					
Mental health and self-harm			✓		✓					
Minority ethnic groups		✓	✓	✓	✓		✓	✓		
Politics		✓	✓	✓	✓		✓	✓		
Poverty				✓	✓					
Pressures and influences	✓				✓	✓				
Rights and perceptions					✓		✓	✓	✓	✓
Sexual health									✓	
Sexual risks							✓	✓	✓	
Social capital	✓	✓	✓	✓	✓	✓	✓	✓	✓	✓
Volunteering								✓		
Young carers								✓		

Table A.2 Mode of survey completion (2003–12 YLT survey)

					Year of survey					
	2003 (%)	2004 (%)	2005 (%)	2006 (%)	2007 (%)	2008 (%)	2009 (%)	2010 (%)	2011 (%)	2012 (%)
Paper	89	98	96	96	95	96	80	85	93	86
Online	9	2	4	4	5	4	20	15	7	14
Telephone	2	1	1	0	0	0	0	0	1	0
Total (n)	902	824	819	772	627	941	856	786	1434	1208
Response rate	46	42	40	39	33	23	23	21	37	32

Getting the data

Tables of results from the survey are available on the YLT website (www.ark.ac.uk/ylt) within six months of the end of the fieldwork period. For each question, results for males and females and also for religious groups can be viewed. These results are also available in the form of pie charts and bar charts. Users who wish to carry out their own statistical analyses can download the data in SPSS portable file format. The questionnaire, as well as technical notes and other publications are also available. In addition, a helpline service is available for anyone who has a query about the survey or the results. The YLT data is also archived with the UK Data Services (http://ukdataservice.ac.uk/)

Contact information

For all queries relating to the survey, please contact:
Dirk Schubotz, YLT Director, School of Sociology, Social Policy and Social Work, Queen's University Belfast, Belfast BT7 1NN. Tel: (028) 9097 3947. Email: d.schubotz@qub.ac.uk

Index

Young people in post-conflict Northern Ireland

The past cannot be changed, but the future can be developed

Edited by Dirk Schubotz and Paula Devine

978-1-905541-34-8

Covers not just what we expect to hear when NI is being discussed: violence, sectarianism, faith-segregated schooling, cross-community contact, politics, peace process. But also: inward migration, mental health, suicide, bullying, pupil participation, sexual health, poverty, class, and how best to find out about these things in robust ways that involve young people in shaping the process. It includes the prize-winning essay from a 16-year old: *Is Anybody Listening?*

'The message of the book is that we have a lot to learn from our youth, if we take the trouble to listen to them' The contribution they make, when they are consulted, can help society with endemic problems such as bullying. The research also shows that the roots of some problems lie in the attitudes young people develop through lack of adequate information.' *Therapy Today*.

Includes:
Shared or scared? Attitudes to community relations among young people 2003–7
  Duncan Morrow
Adolescent mental health in Northern Ireland: empirical evidence from the Young Life and Times Survey
  Katrina Lloyd, Ed Cairns, Claire Doherty & Kate Ellis
Tackling bullying in schools: the role of pupil participation
  Ruth Sinclair
Honesty about sex and relationships – it's not too much to ask for
  Simon Blake
Diversity or diversion? Experiences of education in Northern Ireland
  Tony Gallagher
Young people's thoughts on poverty
  Alex Tennant & Marina Monteith
Is anybody listening?
  Shaun Mulvenna
Giving young people a voice via social research projects: methodological challenges
  Dirk Schubotz & Paula Devine

Reappraisals

Essays in the history of youth and community work

Edited by Ruth Gilchrist, Tony Jeffs, Jean Spence, Naomi Stanton, Aylssa Cowell, Joyce Walker and Tom Wylie

978-1-905541-88-1

The range of material in this volume reflects the editors' hope to encourage practitioners and academics to reflect upon the earlier forms of practice and, via that process, reappraise what they are currently doing within both fieldwork and teaching.

The ten essays include *Scouting in a divided society: Judge William Johnson and the 78th Belfast* by Tom Wylie.

Youthoria

Adolescent substance misuse – problems, prevention and treatment

By Phil Harris

978-1-905541-82-9

'A unique book . . . arguably unrivalled in its scope . . . a work of wisdom and scholarship cleverly combined with a great deal of useful and practical information . . . an engaging, informative and essential read for all professionals working with adolescents.' *British Journal of Social Work*.

'Does a remarkable job in synthesising extensive research findings to provide a comprehensive and coherent framework for understanding and effectively responding to substance use by today's youth . . . a highly readable and engaging book that provides invaluable insights, strategies and tools.' *Professional Social Work*.

'Harris, an independent scholar with years of experience in the field of drug abuse treatment, provides a comprehensive review and analysis of adolescent substance use, associated problems, factors increasing and decreasing the risk of use, and treatment interventions. His perspective on adolescent substance-related issues is refreshing, examining them from within a broader context that includes historical, cultural, social and developmental influences on patterns of use and resulting problems . . . Recognizing that the nature of substance misuse by adolescents differs from that of adults, Harris calls for the use of diagnostic criteria and interventions that reflect the risk factors, paths to problematic use, life consequences, impact of developmental progress, and symptom presentation specific to adolescents. He concludes with a challenge to improve prevention and treatment outcomes of adolescents by applying models informed by current research on developmental processes and practices supported by evidence . . . Highly recommended.' *CHOICE*.